D1288811

Methamphetamine

by Kevin Hillstrom

LUCENT BOOKS
A part of Gale, Cengage Learning

GALE
CENGAGE Learning·

Farmington Hills, Mich • San Francisco • New York • Waterville, Maine
Meriden, Conn • Mason, Ohio • Chicago

LIBRARY OF CONGRESS CATALOGING-IN-PUBLICATION DATA

Hillstrom, Kevin, 1963-
  Methamphetamine / by Kevin Hillstrom
      pages cm. -- (Hot topics)
  Includes bibliographical references and index.
  ISBN 978-1-4205-0872-7 (hardback)
  1. Methamphetamine--United States--Juvenile literature.
  2. Methamphetamine abuse--United States--Juvenile literature.
  I. Title.
  RC568.A45H55 2015
  362.29--dc23
                                        2014019396

Lucent Books
27500 Drake Rd.
Farmington Hills, MI 48331

ISBN-13: 978-1-4205-0872-7
ISBN-10: 1-4205-0872-5

Printed in the United States of America
1 2 3 4 5 6 7 18 17 16 15 14

CONTENTS

FOREWORD

Young people today are bombarded with information. Aside from traditional sources such as newspapers, television, and the radio, they are inundated with a nearly continuous stream of data from electronic media. They send and receive e-mails and instant messages, read and write online blogs, participate in chat rooms and forums, and surf the web for hours. This trend is likely to continue. As Patricia Senn Breivik, the former dean of university libraries at Wayne State University in Detroit, has stated, "Information overload will only increase in the future. By 2020, for example, the available body of information is expected to double every 73 days! How will these students find the information they need in this coming tidal wave of information?"

Ironically, this overabundance of information can actually impede efforts to understand complex issues. Whether the topic is abortion, the death penalty, gay rights, or obesity, the deluge of fact and opinion that floods the print and electronic media is overwhelming. The news media report the results of polls and studies that contradict one another. Cable news shows, talk radio programs, and newspaper editorials promote narrow viewpoints and omit facts that challenge their own political biases. The World Wide Web is an electronic minefield where legitimate scholars compete with the postings of ordinary citizens who may or may not be well informed or capable of reasoned argument. At times, strongly worded testimonials and opinion pieces both in print and electronic media are presented as factual accounts.

Conflicting quotes and statistics can confuse even the most diligent researchers. A good example of this is the question of whether or not the death penalty deters crime. For instance, one study found that murders decreased by nearly one-third when the death penalty was reinstated in New York in 1995. Death penalty supporters cite this finding to support their argument that the existence of the death penalty deters criminals from committing murder. However, another study found that states without the death penalty have murder rates below the national average. This study is cited by opponents of capital punishment, who reject the claim that the death penalty deters murder. Students need context and clear, informed discussion if they are to think critically and make informed decisions.

The Hot Topics series is designed to help young people wade through the glut of fact, opinion, and rhetoric so that they can think critically about controversial issues. Only by reading and thinking critically will they be able to formulate a viewpoint that is not simply the parroted views of others. Each volume of the series focuses on one of today's most pressing social issues and provides a balanced overview of the topic. Carefully crafted narrative, fully documented primary and secondary source quotes, informative sidebars, and study questions all provide excellent starting points for research and discussion. Full-color photographs and charts enhance all volumes in the series. With its many useful features, the Hot Topics series is a valuable resource for young people struggling to understand the pressing issues of the modern era.

INTRODUCTION

A SEDUCTIVE AND DANGEROUS DRUG

Methamphetamine is one of the most poorly understood illegal drugs in the United States. Aside from a brief burst of national attention from news outlets and lawmakers in the early 2000s, it has never received the same level of scrutiny as cocaine, marijuana, or heroin. That relative lack of coverage is usually attributed to the fact that methamphetamine—or meth, as the drug is commonly called—is not used as much as those other drugs. Meth abuse also is strongly associated with rural, working-class white communities that do not always receive as much media attention as the United States' more affluent neighborhoods or more heavily populated urban centers.

Another factor contributing to meth's lower profile is that most Americans have only the haziest understanding of how the drug is produced. Unlike marijuana and cocaine, both of which are produced from naturally occurring plants, meth is a synthetic drug. This means that it is generated by mixing various man-made chemical ingredients together. In fact, Americans' impressions of meth addiction and the criminal meth manufacturing industry arguably have been shaped more by a fictional television drama—AMC's *Breaking Bad*—than by any other information source.

Public health professionals, law enforcement authorities, and recovering addicts warn, however, that an extremely dan-

A chemist from the U.S. Drug Enforcement Administration examines a chunk of crystal methamphetamine.

gerous drug lurks behind this cloud of mystery, ignorance, and Hollywood dramatization. Not only is meth destructive to mind and body, it also is more addictive than either cocaine or heroin. Meth can change brain functions in ways that make it virtually impossible for users to experience happiness without being under the drug's influence. Other symptoms of meth addiction include shocking weight loss, paranoia, hallucinations, days or weeks of sleeplessness, loose and rotted teeth, and permanent damage to vital organs. Any one of these symptoms is capable of disrupting a person's life in negative ways; together they can destroy careers, educational opportunities, marriages, and family relationships within a matter of months.

Law enforcement officials, substance abuse counselors, and other people familiar with the nation's methamphetamine problem also say that the drug is no longer limited to rural parts of the West and Midwest, where it first took root. Propelled by the involvement of Mexican drug cartels and the spread of "do-it-yourself" meth recipes available on the Internet, the drug has infiltrated suburban homes, urban neighborhoods, and fancy apartments in every corner of the United States. This reality, combined with the sheer destructive power of meth addiction, has led many police officers, social workers, and parents to identify methamphetamine as a rising threat to the health and vitality of American families and communities.

THE HISTORY OF METHAMPHETAMINE

The first versions of methamphetamine (meth) were synthesized by German and Japanese chemists in the late nineteenth century. These early concoctions were the first amphetamines, an addictive class of drug that can nonetheless provide energy and a sense of well-being to users.

Meth did not arrive on the global drug scene until 1919. That year, a Japanese chemist named Akira Ogata blended red phosphorus (the active ingredient in matchbook striker pads) and ephedrine, an Asian herbal plant, to create a version of amphetamine that could be dissolved in water. Ogata's methylated (water soluble) version of amphetamine could be absorbed more quickly into the human body than ordinary amphetamine. It also could be injected into the body, unlike non-methylated amphetamine.

A New Wonder Drug

In the 1920s and 1930s doctors prescribed amphetamines to treat a variety of ailments and conditions, including the common cold, fatigue, depression, anxiety, schizophrenia, and asthma. The popularity of amphetamines for these wide-ranging problems was driven by two discoveries about the drugs' effects. First, amphetamines enlarged respiratory passages, which made them appealing decongestants for patients suffering from stuffy noses from colds or allergies. In addition, many patients reported that the drug improved their mood and outlook on life.

By the late 1930s, some physicians in the United States, Japan, and Europe were comparing amphetamines to the "wonder drug" penicillin, an infection-fighting antibiotic that was poised to go into mass production. Their enthusiasm was echoed by pharmaceutical companies that produced huge volumes of the drugs in pill and inhaler form. Another factor in the steadily growing popularity of amphetamines was that users often reported diminished appetite. This side effect attracted the attention of women who wanted to lose weight.

When World War II raged across Europe and the Pacific from 1939 to 1945, armies on both sides of the conflict freely distributed methamphetamine and other types of amphetamines to their troops. American, Japanese, British, and German commanders all relied on the drugs to boost the energy and alertness of their troops. They also sometimes distributed them to soldiers

Amphetamine, shown here in a three-dimensional computer model, became widely used in the 1920s and 1930s for its ability to cure a variety of ailments.

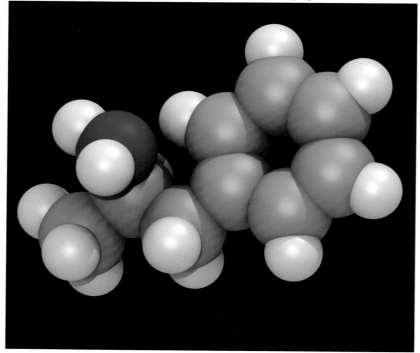

as a way to reduce their hunger and thus stretch limited food supplies.

By the time the war ended, though, researchers had uncovered troubling indications that methamphetamine and other stimulants in the amphetamine drug family had the potential to be highly addictive. Reports began to surface of users who became depressed, angry, or agitated when deprived of the drug. Historians also noted that German dictator Adolf Hitler, whose actions had plunged the world into World War II, received regular injections of meth during the war's final years. This knowledge has led to speculation that the drug might have worsened Hitler's well-documented mental instability and paranoia.

"Mother's Little Helper"

Once the war ended, amphetamine drug production ceased in Japan and other nations stopped handing out amphetamines to their soldiers. But these countries still possessed huge amounts of the drug, and many servicemen had become dependent on amphetamines. In the U.S. military alone, as many as 16 million men were exposed to amphetamines during the war.[1] Almost overnight, postwar Japan, Europe, and the United States all experienced a surge in illegal black market sales of amphetamines.

Meanwhile, legal manufacture of amphetamines continued to grow. During the 1950s, the drugs became particularly popular with people who needed to stay awake and productive for long periods, including long-haul truckers, college students cramming for final exams, and factory workers pulling long shifts. Stay-at-home moms also used them in large quantities. "Amphetamines came to be called 'mother's little helper,' both because they were handy appetite suppressants and because mothers could pop these pills to become peppier housewives," writes Olivia Dahl in the *Dartmouth Undergraduate Journal of Science*. "In 1962, amphetamine use was so prevalent that there were eight billion amphetamine tablets circulating in America alone."[2]

In 1960 the first methamphetamine inhaler became commercially available. It sparked another huge wave of meth use, even after a 1965 law changed the inhaler from an over-the-counter drug to one that required a prescription from a doctor. "Thirty-one million prescriptions were written in 1967, mostly for women," says drug expert Patricia Case of Harvard University. "Methamphetamine was seen as a women's drug . . . for weight loss and an antidepressant. And I think that most meth users will tell you, that's exactly their experience."[3] Case adds that meth's mood-lifting properties were especially seductive to women who felt trapped as homemakers during the conservative 1950s and early 1960s.

LIVES SPIRALING OUT OF CONTROL

"Crystal meth may make people feel good for a while but then it totally destroys folks. People get agitated and paranoid and are screaming and shouting. They can stay up for days without eating and not take care of their kids. They often get in terrible car accidents."—Matthew Frances, an emergency room doctor in California

Quoted in Ioan Grillo. "Mexican Meth Production Goes on Speed." Reuters, May 10, 2012. www.reuters.com/article/2012/05/10/us-mexico-drugs-meth-idUSBRE84908 820120510.

All during this period, though, the black market for amphetamines remained alive and well. People who could not obtain or afford a doctor's prescription stole them or bought them from dealers who forged prescriptions, set up fake companies to order the drugs from overseas factories, or smuggled tablets into the United States.

Criminal Trade in Meth Increases

Public concern about drug abuse soared during the 1960s. This was an enormously turbulent decade in American history, marked by titanic struggles over civil rights for minori-

Many young people in the 1960s embraced the "hippie movement" and experimented with drugs such as LSD, marijuana, cocaine, and amphetamines—also commonly called speed.

ties, the Vietnam War, sexual behavior, and the responsibilities and rights of women. Many young people and other Americans who rebelled against "traditional" American life embraced consciousness-altering illegal drugs such as marijuana, LSD, and heroin. Abuse of amphetamines, which came to be popularly known as speed, also escalated during this time.

Policymakers and law enforcement authorities tried to stamp out the market for these drugs with new laws targeting people who manufactured, sold, or used illegal substances. Amphetamines were the focus of some of these drug laws, but cocaine and heroin were the biggest targets. Those hard drugs were much more closely associated with crime, violence, and deadly overdoses than amphetamines, which could still be obtained through a doctor's prescription. In addition, many Americans still viewed amphetamines primarily as an aid for work or school, not as potentially dangerous drugs.

In 1965 Congress imposed the first federal restrictions on the manufacture of amphetamines. Five years later, the 1970 Comprehensive Drug Abuse Prevention and Control Act was signed into law. This sweeping legislation established amphetamines as Class II controlled substances, meaning that their sale and possession came under broad new restrictions. Under these new rules, amphetamine users required a fresh prescription each time they acquired a supply of the drug. In addition, doctors and pharmacists had to keep detailed records of amphetamine prescriptions or face prosecution. Prescription sales of amphetamines and related drugs dropped dramatically as soon as the new law came into effect.

When authorities moved to curtail the legal trade in amphetamines, however, they unintentionally opened another door. "By cutting the legal supply to a trickle, the government signaled to drug dealers—and would-be drug dealers—that they could collect substantial profits from an established clientele if they started manufacturing amphetamines,"[4] explains journalist Jack Shafer.

The first criminal operations to take advantage of the expanded black market in amphetamines were outlaw motorcycle gangs in San Diego County and other parts of California. These gangs had already established underground production sites for meth and other types of amphetamines in the 1960s. As the money from amphetamine trafficking began to roll in, they were joined by other criminals eager to cash in on the drug.

The Rise of Crystal Meth

These illegal amphetamine trafficking operations did not attract much attention in the 1970s. Authorities, public health officials, and news media outlets focused almost all of their attention on heroin, cocaine, marijuana, and other illegal drugs. In the 1980s, though, demand for product from meth cooking operations jumped in some regions of the West.

The key to this sudden surge was the development of a new version of methamphetamine known as crystal meth. In 1980 federal authorities placed tough new restrictions on a chemical called Phenyl-2-propanone (P2P), which had been the precursor, or key ingredient, in the amphetamine-cooking operations of the biker gangs. In their search for a substitute for P2P, traffickers discovered that ephedrine—an ingredient found in everyday nasal decongestants—could be used to make crystal meth, a crystalline form of the drug that was much more powerful and addictive than its predecessors.

Once ephedrine became an ingredient in meth-making operations, the nation's troubles with the wide family of drugs known as amphetamines evolved primarily into a struggle against meth. "It's pretty much like a high-octane gasoline versus a low-octane gasoline," explains Rob Bovett, a narcotics enforcement officer in Oregon. "Methamphetamine, of course, is the high-octane version."[5]

Home-Brewed Meth in the Heartland

During the 1980s and early 1990s, meth production expanded gradually from California into other western states and then into the Midwest. Many factors contributed to this expansion

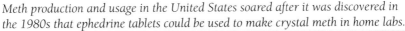

Meth production and usage in the United States soared after it was discovered in the 1980s that ephedrine tablets could be used to make crystal meth in home labs.

besides the increased potency of crystal meth. One was the ease with which traffickers could obtain mass quantities of ephedrine for cooking up new batches of meth. Another was the growing involvement of veteran drug trafficking organizations from Mexico. These outfits began sending ever-greater volumes of crystal meth along the same distribution pipelines they had built during the 1970s and 1980s to sell cocaine, heroin, and marijuana across the United States. Unlike those illegal drugs, however, the Mexican cartels did not have to take the risk of transporting meth over the border. Since all the ingredients for making meth could be easily obtained in the United States, the cartels started establishing their own "meth kitchens" in remote corners of California.

They were not the only people making crystal meth, though. Ordinary Americans from all walks of life manufactured meth on a much smaller scale, either to sell or to satisfy their own cravings for the drug. They were able to do this because ephedrine was easy and inexpensive to obtain. So were the other ingredients used in various meth recipes in circulation at that time, including paint thinner, acetone, battery acid, and anhydrous ammonia, a common agricultural fertilizer.

Producing small quantities of meth did not require fancy or expensive facilities, either. Batches could be made in a matter of a few hours in household kitchens, bathrooms, and hotel rooms. These operations were extremely dangerous, however. They became notorious for claiming lives in explosions and causing serious burns and other health problems for adults and children exposed to meth chemicals.

Law enforcement agencies detected a huge boom in "do-it-yourself" or "home-brewed" meth operations across the Great Plains and the Midwest—the country's so-called heartland—in the late 1980s and early 1990s. They attributed this jump in part to the simple meth production process and the highly addictive nature of the drug. But it also stemmed from wrenching socioeconomic changes that rocked countless farming communities in Iowa, Kansas, Missouri, Nebraska, Oklahoma, and other rural

The Queen of Meth

One of the most notorious meth dealers in American history is Lori Arnold, the sister of comedian and actor Tom Arnold. Born in Ottumwa, Iowa, in 1961, Arnold dropped out of high school and married Floyd Stockdall, a motorcycle gang member with links to meth producers in California. In the late 1980s Arnold established a small meth trafficking business in her home state. Within a matter of a few years, she had created the biggest meth production and distribution network in the entire Midwest.

Arnold used the drug money to buy herself a horse ranch, a car dealership, and fourteen houses. "I had everything," she recalled. "The cars, the clubs, the money. I even bought a plane, just because I could." It all came crashing down in 1990, though, when she was arrested by the FBI. She served the next eight years in prison, leaving behind a ten-year-old son.

After her release from prison, Arnold quickly drifted back into the meth trade. She was sent back to prison in 2001. Since her 2008 release, Arnold has worked at a telephone call center in Phoenix and has remarried, this time to a trucker named John Woten. She seems untroubled about her drug-dealing past. "I had some friends who got hooked on my meth, and they went down the tubes," she said. "Yeah, I probably ruined a few lives. Sometimes I feel guilty. But I made millions of dollars and I had a blast doing it."

Jeff Maysh. "The Adventures of America's Original Meth Queen." The Fix.com, March 21, 2011. www.thefix.com/content/how-americas-meth-queen-melted-down?page=all.

states in the 1980s. Falling crop prices forced many family farms out of business. At the same time, powerful corporations acquired meatpacking plants, dairy operations, feedlots, and other locally owned businesses that traditionally had provided good, decent-paying jobs in rural communities. The new owners often slashed the size of the work force at these facilities and cut the wages and benefits of those workers who remained. When the giant Cargill corporation bought a meatpacking plant in Ottumwa, Iowa, in 1987, for example, it laid off two-thirds of the plant's workers and cut wages from $18 an hour to $5.60 an hour with no benefits.[6]

All of these blows battered small towns and families that traditionally had relied on farming and other agriculture-related activities for their economic well-being. Young people who might have stayed in the community to work the family farm or take a stable job at the local meatpacking plant fled out of state in search of better opportunities.

Many of the residents who remained felt like they had no choice but to work longer hours or take second jobs in order to make ends meet. "The real story [of meth's rise] is as much about the death of a way of life as it is about the birth of a drug," writes journalist Nick Reding. Growing numbers of working-class men and women in the country's heartland first experimented with meth because they heard that it boosted energy and lifted feelings of anxiety and depression. "Meatpacking workers hoping to stay awake long enough to take on double shifts bought the drug in increasing quantities," explains Reding. "[Working-class Americans] were able to get a stronger form of meth at a much better price—this at a time when the drug's effects were arguably more useful than ever. . . . Meth [became] much more widely available at exactly the moment that rural economies collapsed and people left."[7]

Flawed Efforts to Curb Meth Production

In the mid-1980s the Drug Enforcement Administration (DEA), the leading federal agency responsible for enforcing American drug laws, urged Congress to pass new laws to monitor and restrict the sale of ephedrine, the main ingredient in meth. The pharmaceutical industry, however, convinced influential members of Congress to block the DEA's proposals. The industry claimed that new regulations would reduce their profits and force them to raise prices on asthma medication and diet pills that contained ephedrine.

In 1988 Congress finally agreed to pass new regulations to track imports of ephedrine, which is produced in only nine factories around the world (none in the United States). But the big drug companies convinced Congress to include an important exception to the new monitoring law: only shipments of ephedrine in powder form would be tracked. The law imposed no monitoring requirements on ephedrine that was imported in pill form. This provision was a big help to the meth industry. "All that meth manufacturers had to do in order to continue making the drug would be legally to buy pill-form ephedrine in bulk

Drug Enforcement Administration (DEA) agents photograph evidence taken from a meth lab in Ohio in 2004. Since the 1980s, the DEA has put pressure on Congress to regulate easily accessible ingredients that can be used to make meth.

and crush it into powder—a small, added inconvenience,"[8] explains Reding.

In the early 1990s doctors in many western and midwestern states reported increased levels of crystal meth addiction in their communities. Local, state, and federal law enforcement agencies all warned that meth labs were expanding in size and number as well. In 1993 the DEA finally convinced Congress to pass a new federal law that eliminated the ephedrine pill exception. The nine factories that produced ephedrine also agreed to new tracking measures for the precursor chemical. As a result of these new monitoring practices, Mexican drug cartels and small-time meth cooks alike found it much more difficult to obtain ephedrine.

Within a matter of months, however, meth operations found an effective substitute for ephedrine—pseudoephedrine, the dominant ingredient in Nyquil, Sudafed, and other cold and flu medicines. This development was a nightmare for the DEA and other agencies and organizations fighting meth. Supplies of "pseudo," as pseudoephedrine is often called, were plentiful. Not only was it used in many of America's most popular non-prescription medicines, it also had been excluded from the various laws that finally corralled ephedrine. And since pseudo-based cold medicines generated huge amounts of revenue for American drug companies, the DEA knew that it would be enormously difficult to pass new restrictions on the sale of psuedo-based cold medicines. Drug companies would see any such proposals as a threat to the profitability of their most important products. Perhaps worst of all, though, the new pseudo-based meth recipes made the drug even more powerful and addictive.

America Wakes Up to the Meth Epidemic

In the late 1990s and early 2000s meth abuse continued its steady growth. It became a public health menace in towns and neighborhoods of all shapes and sizes. In San Francisco, for example, public health officials warned that meth had infiltrated the city's large gay community to an alarming degree. Doctors

Meth in the Big City

Most of the attention given to meth has revolved around its devastating impact on rural communities. But it has also taken a heavy toll in some large metropolitan areas. In San Francisco, for example, crystal meth addiction became a serious public health issue for the city's large gay community in the 1990s and early 2000s. "I used to have the house and the Mercedes and the big job," recalled one gay man who worked in the city as a lawyer. "Then I fell into crystal. Oh, my God, it was great. I felt young and powerful and wonderful. . . . [But] crystal destroyed my life. I sold everything I could put my hands on [to buy more meth]. What I didn't sell, I lost: my house, my career. The more I used it, the more I needed it. . . . Crystal tells your brain to go back and get more, more, more. The logical side of your mind is saying, 'I can't keep doing this,' but you are still on your way to the dealer's house."

Michael Specter. "Higher Risk: Crystal Meth, the Internet, and Dangerous Choices about AIDS." *New Yorker*, May 23, 2005. www.newyorker.com/archive /2005/05/23/050523fa_fact.

and police in small towns across the middle of the country reported that their emergency rooms and local jails were filling up with meth addicts, some of whom turned to robbery or prostitution to feed their addictions.

Yet meth's growth into a truly national problem continued to go largely unrecognized until 2004 and 2005. The first major news coverage of meth was an investigative series written by journalist Steve Suo for *The Oregonian* in 2004. It was soon followed by high-profile stories on the "meth epidemic" by national magazines, television networks, and major newspapers. The American public expressed shock at these reports, which revealed that meth's grip was strongest in rural, mostly white communities that were not usually associated with narcotics-related crimes or drug addiction.

The police officers, nurses, doctors, and addicts who were interviewed in these stories described meth as a dark force that was ripping families and communities apart. "Meth is the single most serious law enforcement issue that North Dakota is facing, and has ever faced," said that state's attorney general in a 2004 interview with the *New York Times*. In the same article, a drug investigator in central Nebraska asserted, "we never had a big crime problem in Nebraska till meth. But now we have a lot of stabbings and shootings in our little towns and every homicide goes back to meth."[9]

The Combat Methamphetamine Epidemic Act of 2005

The wave of news coverage about the United States' meth problems also described the various loopholes that Congress had placed in the anti-meth laws it had passed in the 1990s. Stung by accusations that they had paid more attention to drug companies than to meth-threatened families in crafting those laws, federal lawmakers passed the Combat Methamphetamine Epidemic Act in 2005. The legislation, also known as the Combat Meth Act, was patterned after strong anti-meth laws passed by Oregon and Oklahoma in 2004. It was signed into law by President George W. Bush on March 9, 2006.

The Combat Meth Act contained several important provisions. First, it called for halting foreign aid to any country that failed to control and carefully monitor its purchases of ephedrine and pseudoephedrine. This measure convinced Mexico, home of North America's biggest meth cartels, to severely restrict the import of both chemicals. The law also placed new restrictions on the amount of pseudo and ephedrine that U.S. drug companies could bring into the country.

The provisions of the Combat Meth Act that attracted the most attention, though, were those that set a limit on the amount of cold medicine that American consumers could purchase at their local pharmacies. Specifically, the act required all cold medicines and other products containing pseudoephedrine to be placed behind pharmacy sales counters. It also required pharmacies to start electronically tracking each and every sale of these cold medicines. Under this system, pharmacies had a legal

Michigan senator John Proos speaks to a pharmacist about new regulations on pseudoephedrine, a medical drug used to make meth that was put under strict monitoring under the Combat Meth Act.

responsibility to disallow sales of cold medicine to customers who reached a monthly purchase limit.

This so-called stop-buy provision was included over strong objections from the National Association of Retail Chain Stores, which represented CVS, Walgreens, Rite-Aid, Wal-Mart, and other big drugstore chains. These companies wanted to continue the same practices they had been following for years—to sell cold medicine without any restrictions and pass along handwritten sales data to law enforcement authorities after the fact. The drug chains protested that the new law forced them to act as policemen of sorts. Veteran DEA official Tony Loya rejected this complaint, though. "Does refusing the sale of alcohol and tobacco to minors amount to 'policing'?" he said. "Yes, it does. And the drug chains have been doing that without complaint for years. So what's the difference if they have to tell a few people that they can't buy more than a certain amount of Sudafed?"[10]

Signs of Progress

Many observers believe that the Combat Meth Act struck a significant blow to meth traffickers. After the law was passed, Pfizer, the world's largest maker of cold medicine, eliminated pseudo from its products. The company replaced it with a DEA-approved chemical called phenylephrine, which cannot be used to make meth. Pfizer's decision reduced worldwide production of pseudo, which made it harder for meth cooks to get their hands on the drug. Some researchers assert, however, that phenylephrine-based medicines are not as effective at relieving cold symptoms as pseudo-based drugs.

WAITING TOO LONG BEFORE ACTING

"You don't want to be too far *behind* the curve [in enacting federal drug abuse policies]. . . . Then, you end up missing it, like we did with crystal meth. We missed that one on a national level, but if you were in a little town in Iowa, and you're devastated by meth, you don't really care what the national data tells you."
—Gil Kerlikowske, Commissioner of U.S. Customs and Border Protection and former director of the Office of National Drug Control Policy

Quoted in Mike Guy. "Interview with the Drug Czar." The Fix.com, July 2, 2012. www .thefix.com/content/interview-drug-czar-gil-kerlikowske7459?page=all.

State and local law enforcement authorities also reported big declines in raids on do-it-yourself meth labs in the nation's heartland. They said that home-brewed meth labs were drying up because the cooks could no longer secure the necessary ingredients. Meanwhile, major studies of illegal drug use conducted by the National Institute of Drug Abuse (NIDA) and the University of Michigan's Monitoring the Future survey indicated a small but steady drop in meth use across the United States in the mid-2000s. NIDA also reported a notable downturn in the percentage of workers across the country who tested positive for meth. These findings led John Walters, director of the Office of

National Drug Control Policy, to state in June 2006 that "communities once paralyzed by the threat of this dangerous drug are emerging healthier and safer because we have reduced the diversion of precursor chemicals and the number of meth labs."[11]

Other officials admitted that meth abuse remained a major public health concern. But they still expressed relief that small-time meth cooks were being squeezed out of business by the new state and federal laws. "Demand [for meth is still] being met by trafficking from other states or Mexico," reported Tom Cunningham of the Oklahoma Drug Task Force. At the same time, though, he said that his state's anti-meth initiatives reduced meth lab raids by 80 to 90 percent in the space of two years. "What we don't have [anymore] are these deathtrap labs, destroying property and putting kids at risk."[12]

Trends in Mexican Meth Production

Since the mid-2000s passage of the Combat Meth Act, Mexican meth production has grown. As a result, Mexican drug cartels account for a steadily growing share of the total meth consumed in the United States. The cartels have learned to work around Mexico's efforts to halt the stream of meth ingredients flowing into the country. Criminal gangs either smuggle in the precursor chemicals or import them through fake companies that seem legitimate on the surface. The ingredients are then transported to labs capable of generating massive volumes of cheap and highly addictive meth for distribution across Mexico and the United States. "These are sophisticated, high-tech operations in Mexico that are operating with extreme precision," says one DEA agent based in Missouri. "They're moving it out the door as fast as they can manufacture it."[13]

Law enforcement agencies have intercepted ever higher amounts of meth at the Mexico–United States border in recent years. Border seizures by the DEA, the U.S. Border Patrol, and other agencies jumped from 4,000 pounds of meth (1,814kg) in 2007 to 16,000 pounds (7,257kg) in 2011.[14] Raids on meth labs deep in Mexico have also increased. In early 2012 Mexican

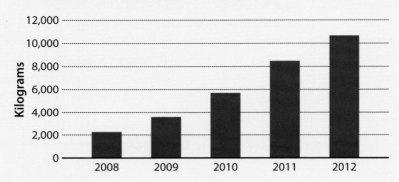

SEIZURES OF METHAMPHETAMINE AT THE UNITED STATES–MEXICO BORDER

The amount of methamphetamine seized each year entering the United States at the southwestern border has increased dramatically in recent years.

Source: U.S. Department of Justice Drug Enforcement Administration. *National Drug Threat Assessment Summary 2013*, November 2013, p. 5. www.justice.gov /dea/resource-center/DIR-017-13%20NDTA%20Summary%20final.pdf.

soldiers seized 15 tons (15,000kg) of crystal meth worth about $1.2 billion in a single raid on a lab in western Mexico, outside the city of Guadalajara.[15] But officials fear that the volume of meth that is being successfully smuggled across the border into American towns and cities is rising, too. "We are a victim of our own success," says one U.S. anti-narcotics special agent based in Arizona. "When you look at domestic meth labs, those numbers have fallen off the table. But where have they gone? Mexico."[16]

Efforts to combat these Mexico-based operations include reducing demand for meth in U.S. communities. In that regard, statistical trends in meth use offer some hopeful signs. In 2011 the Substance Abuse and Mental Health Services Administration published a national survey on U.S. drug, alcohol, and tobacco use. It found that the number of monthly meth users across the nation declined from 731,000 Americans (0.3 percent of the total U.S. population) in 2006 to 439,000 (0.2 percent) in 2011.[17] A 2013 Monitoring the Future survey of adolescent drug use reported that the percentage of American twelfth-graders who reported using meth at least once in the previous year plummeted from 4.7 percent in 1999 to 1.1 percent in 2012.[18]

The Rise of Shake and Bake

Law enforcement authorities and public health experts are very concerned, however, about the arrival and spread of a so-called "shake and bake" method of meth production. Under this simple process, meth users who can get their hands on pseudoephedrine-based cold and allergy medicines are able to synthesize their own cheap and potent supply of the drug. According to journalist Jonah Engle, shake and bake operations expanded meth production well beyond "the province of people

A large pile of illegal drugs, including heroin, marijuana, and meth, is burned by a soldier at a military base in Monterrey, Mexico.

with *Breaking Bad*-style knowledge of chemistry. . . . If anyone wondered what would happen if heroin or cocaine addicts suddenly discovered how to make their own supply with a handful of cheap ingredients readily available over the counter, methamphetamine's recent history provides an answer."[19]

Many public health and law enforcement officials worry that the increasing popularity of shake and bake, combined with the growing volume of Mexican meth, could generate higher levels of meth abuse in rural areas of the West, Midwest, and South. Some drug enforcement agents believe that the foundations for a new meth epidemic may even be forming. "I think that you are going to see an increase in meth abuse nationwide," said one DEA agent in Phoenix, Arizona, in 2012. "With the amount that's coming across [the border from Mexico], it's definitely a concern."[20]

METH'S TOLL
ON USERS

Law enforcement officials, public health experts, and medical researchers agree that methamphetamine is one of the most frightening drugs in circulation around the world. Meth's fearsome reputation stems in part from the way that it lures people into addiction. Not only does meth provide an initial sense of euphoria and well-being to first-time users, it also possesses strong physically addictive properties. Criminal drug syndicates and small-time meth cooks alike have exploited these effects to turn millions of people in the United States and around the world into desperate buyers of their product.

But police officers, doctors, and addiction experts also talk about meth in such grim tones because of the ways that the drug damages—and in some cases destroys—the physical health of people who use it regularly. They all tell stories of users whose addictions have turned their mouths into decaying messes and their minds into fog banks of hallucination and memory loss.

Key Meth Ingredients

Methamphetamine is known by a wide variety of names on the street, including speed, crank, chalk, crystal, glass, ice, spackle, stove top, trash, tina, and zip. In some cases, these different names reflect different forms of meth that are produced using different recipes. The drug can be smoked, injected, swallowed, or inhaled up the nose, depending on how it is prepared. The most potent and purest form of the drug is crystal meth, which is also known as crystal, glass, and ice because it takes the form of clear shards of icy material. Crystal meth reminds some people of pieces of chandelier.

The key ingredients that give meth its tremendous punch are ephedrine or pseudoephedrine. "Ephedrine and pseudoephedrine are to methamphetamine what flour is to bread—THE essential ingredient,"[21] states the office of Illinois Attorney General Lisa Madigan. These legitimate drug compounds are the main active ingredients in many cold, allergy, and cough medicines. But when these so-called precursor chemicals are mixed and processed with certain other chemicals, the resulting mixture becomes methamphetamine.

Ingredients used in combination with ephedrine or pseudoephedrine to make meth can be found in products used every day in homes and small businesses or on farms. They include red phosphorus (taken from road flares and matchbook covers), lithium (from batteries), toluene (from brake cleaner), and anhydrous ammonia (contained in fertilizers). Other common ingredients found in meth recipes, which can be easily found on the Internet, include ammonia, drain cleaner, iodine, battery acid, antifreeze, salt, and camp stove fuel. The strength and toxicity of cooked batches of meth can vary sig-

Some of the ingredients to make meth are displayed on a table. The ease of procuring ingredients has made home-cooked meth increasingly common.

nificantly, depending on which recipe is followed and the skill of the cook.

Drug experts are also issuing warnings about the revival of a third type of meth production based on the drug phenylacetone. This chemical can be made into phenyl-2-propanone—known in the meth industry as P2P—which can in turn be made into meth. The P2P method of production was used in the 1960s and 1970s by some of the outlaw biker gangs who first launched the meth trade in the United States. It quickly fell out of favor after U.S. lawmakers choked off the phenylacetone supply and meth cooks discovered that they could make large quantities of highly addictive meth using ephedrine and pseudoephedrine. When regulations on the distribution and sale of ephedrine and pseudo were tightened in the 1990s and early 2000s, though, P2P meth began making a comeback. Although phenylacetone is still tightly regulated in the United States, it is easily obtainable in Mexico. Drug cartels operating in Mexico have thus returned to this "old school" method of meth production. In 2012, officials with the U.S. Drug Enforcement Agency estimated that 85 percent of the meth they seized in late 2011 came from the P2P process—a 35 percent increase from 2010.[22]

Meth Kitchens and Superlabs

Do-it-yourself meth makers can cook up small batches for personal use or sale using a variety of inexpensive items that can be obtained at local hardware and home improvement stores. This equipment includes camp stoves, aquarium pumps, rubber tubing, mason jars and other glassware, and Pyrex dishes. The big drug cartels that maintain "superlabs" in Mexico and California's sprawling Central Valley, however, rely on commercial-grade laboratory equipment to generate huge volumes of meth. According to some experts, a single superlab can churn out 1 million or more doses of meth over the course of a single weekend.

Meth is generally cooked in stages that take about twenty-four to forty-eight hours to complete, although some primitive

Signs of a Meth Lab

Law enforcement officials observe that local meth-cooking facilities often have certain characteristics in common. One of the prevailing signs of meth production is a strong and offensive odor around a structure. This odor is often compared to the smell of cat urine or rotten eggs, and it is one of the primary reasons that meth-cooking operations are so often found in remote rural areas or abandoned urban neighborhoods.

Another indication that a building contains a meth lab is the presence of large amounts of trash—especially cold medication packaging; stained coffee filters or bed sheets with powdery residue; empty containers of chemicals such as starter fluid, antifreeze, paint thinner, and white gas; plastic or rubber hoses; duct tape; rubber gloves and respiratory masks; and plastic soda bottles with holes in them.

Other indications that a home, garage, or other building might be a meth-cooking site include blackened or covered windows; security measures, including guard dogs, video cameras, and "Keep Out" signs; sections of burned grass or vegetation where toxic chemicals have been dumped; and frequent visitors and other activity late at night.

A house that had been used as a meth lab is demolished in Albuquerque, New Mexico. Once a house is used for meth production, the amount of toxic residue often makes the structure unlivable.

fastened directly to the body of the bike. Another popular shaking method involves driving around with the bottles in a car with the windows down. Both the bike and car preparation options have the added benefit of dispersing the nasty and distinctive smell of the chemical reactions that produce meth.

A FORMER METH COOK LOOKS BACK

"I can look back and see the total devastation of all that I created, and the lives affected, the houses that I destroyed. . . . It's like a whirlpool. Once you get caught in the current, you just go around and around and around. And pretty soon, it just takes you under. And you've got to come through the other side. But the insanity's got to stop somewhere in order for those things to take place."—former meth lab operator and dealer Robert Lucier

Quoted in "The Meth Epidemic: Transcript." *FRONTLINE: The Meth Epidemic.* PBS, May 2011. www.pbs.org/wgbh/pages/frontline/meth/etc/script.html.

Although the shake and bake method does not use a heat source, the chemicals used are highly combustible when mixed together. One wrong or unlucky move and the bottle can turn into a fireball capable of disfiguring or even killing both users and innocent bystanders. Law enforcement agents relate incidents in which bottles have exploded simply because their tops have been unscrewed too quickly. "You're mixing things that are never designed to be put together, strong acids and bases, drain cleaners and engine starters, things like that, that are never supposed to be put into the same bottle," explains a state district attorney in Oregon. "So it's incredibly dangerous to do. But when you're strung out on meth, you're willing to do a lot of crazy things."[25]

The final product is also extremely dangerous. Shake and bake is such a primitive method for creating meth that it typically leaves a high percentage of toxic chemicals in the final product. Whether these chemicals are smoked, injected, or snorted, they can seriously damage the health of shake and bake users.

Highly Addictive to Both Mind and Body

Meth's record of luring people into long and self-destructive addictions is rooted in the intense, euphoric high that users experience when they first try the drug. "It gave me a sense of power,"
recalls one middle-aged meth user from New York. "It was like
all the switches in my body and my brain felt like they finally got
turned on."[26] Meth also can provide a range of appealing short-
term benefits, including weight loss, more intense sexual experi-
ences, and increased energy for taking care of tasks at work or
at home.

These effects all stem from the fact that methamphetamine
is a central nervous system stimulant. Specifically, meth stimu-
lates the human brain to release dopamine, a natural chemical
that is associated with feelings of happiness and pleasure. Also,

A drug user smokes crystal meth from a makeshift pipe made from a light bulb.

A Father's Misery

In 2008 journalist David Sheff published *Beautiful Boy*, a memoir about his son Nic's harrowing addiction to crystal methamphetamine. In the book, Sheff admitted that Nic's addiction nearly tore their family apart. It also made the author feel so guilt-ridden and heartbroken that he sometimes wished that he could forget that he ever had a son: "It got so bad I wanted to wipe out and delete and expunge every trace of him from my brain so that I would not have to worry about him anymore and I would not have to be disappointed by him and hurt by him and I would not have to blame myself and blame him and I would no longer have the relentless and haunting slide show of images of my lovely son, drugged, in the most sordid, horrible scenes imaginable. . . . I was in wretched anguish and yearned for relief."

Nic eventually kicked his meth addiction with the help of his family. He became actively involved in helping other people struggling with meth addiction, and he has written two books about his journey out of addiction.

David Sheff. *Beautiful Boy: A Father's Journey Through His Son's Addiction.* New York: Houghton Mifflin, 2008, p. 241.

David Sheff (right) appears with his son Nic at an event for his book, Beautiful Boy, about Nic's struggle with meth addiction.

unlike other illegal drugs such as cocaine, the high associated with meth can last for several hours. "It was mind-blowing," recalls Lauren, a Kansas teen who first tried meth when she was fifteen years old. "I felt weightless and had a smile from ear to ear. I was addicted right after that first time."[27]

Regular meth users quickly find, however, that it takes more and more of the drug to experience the long-lasting high they enjoyed so much. Their bodies build up a tolerance for the drug, which means that users have to take larger doses at more frequent intervals to recapture those euphoric feelings. "The body actually forms antibodies, effectively vaccinating itself against the drug and thereby making the 'high' increasingly difficult to achieve," explains journalist Nick Reding. "The more meth [users consume], the more difficult it is to get high."[28] This pattern has been confirmed by addicts such as Amber, who began using meth when she was only twelve years old. "At the beginning I was taking one pill, but then I started needing a whole vial to get the effect."[29]

Meth habits can thus become expensive very quickly. "The daily costs for meth users vary according to personal tolerances and frequency of use," observe criminology scholars at Southeast Missouri State University:

> [But] heavily addicted users indicate they spend as much as $400 a day to meet their habit. . . . The obvious question becomes where do they get their money? Very few can afford that kind of habit and even fewer can afford it without changing their lifestyle. Meth addiction generates property crime and thus costs the public in terms of losses and increased enforcement.[30]

Behavioral Side Effects of Meth Addiction

Medical studies of meth addiction have established that the drug often takes a severe and lasting toll on the emotional well-being of regular users. As *The Oregonian* observed in a well-known 2004 investigative report on the nation's meth crisis:

Meth is the ultimate fool's gold among illicit drugs. It makes users feel euphoric, confident, intelligent, energetic, and sexually desirable. But, over time, it steals those very attributes, making users depressed, insecure, confused, tired, and impotent. Once addicted, users struggle to feel pleasure without the drug.[31]

Researchers say that this phenomenon develops because regular meth use actually changes the structure of regions of the brain that are responsible for feelings and emotions. First, methamphetamine exhausts the body's stores of dopamine. It then interferes with the brain's ability to replenish the lost dopamine. Over time, it becomes more and more difficult for users to experience pleasure and avoid periods of deep depression without the artificial stimulation of meth. "Everything feels kind of gray and hopeless and nothing feels good," explains drug expert Richard Rawson. "And so, in their mind, the only way they're going to feel better is to take more methamphetamine, and hence you

A brain scan with dopamine receptors highlighted shows the devastating effect of meth on the brain's pleasure centers, as it depletes the brain's ability to create enough dopamine.

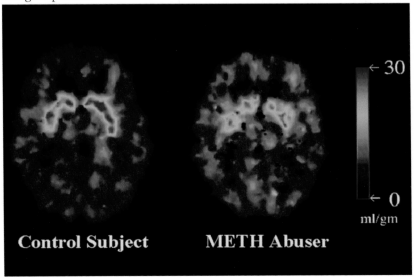

have relapse and people going back to using. It's a wonder any meth users ever get better."[32]

Scientists say that the dopamine levels of people who manage to kick their meth addictions can recover over time and return to more normal levels. In other respects, however, prolonged abuse of meth can permanently damage the brain. Studies report permanent losses in judgment, motor skills, and memory among heavy meth users. Addicts in the grip of meth-fueled highs, meanwhile, frequently experience a frightening array of mental problems that worsen over time. These problems include deep feelings of paranoia, confusion, and bizarre hallucinations. For example, doctors report that meth addicts who come in for treatment sometimes have scabs and sores all over their bodies. They inflict these wounds on themselves by scratching at imaginary insects—sometimes called crank bugs—they believe are crawling under their skin.

People high on meth also exhibit a diminished ability to control sexual urges. This places even casual users at higher risk of engaging in sexually risky behavior, such as unprotected sex with strangers for pleasure, money, or additional doses of meth. Doctors and law enforcement officials also report elevated rates of sexual assault against friends and young family members by meth addicts.

THEY LOOKED LIKE SKELETONS

"[My friends] were completely different people on meth. They looked like skeletons."—Lauren, who began using meth when she was fifteen years old

Quoted in Julie Mehta. "Dark Crystal: Meet Three Young People Who Got Swept Up in Meth Madness." *Current Health 2*, November 2005, p. 16. http://juliemehta.com/health_files/CHmeth.pdf.

Another common symptom of a meth-based high is hyperactive behavior that can continue for hours or even days at a time. This phenomenon is known as tweaking. "Meth addicts' minds are racing, overstimulated—they get tremendous reward by doing the same thing over and over," explains Alex Stalcup, director of a California-based meth addiction rehabilitation center. "I've watched people take apart clocks and sewing machines by the hour. . . . They can't stop. If they pull out of it, they feel negative in a minute."[33] Health experts also warn that tweaking can result in severe levels of sleep deprivation that can add to the emotional and physical stress under which the addict is operating.

Meth also can dramatically erode the physical health of heavy users in other ways. People under the influence of meth are at greater risk of suffering strokes and heart attacks, for instance, because the drug triggers constriction of blood vessels, increased heart rates, and spikes in blood pressure. The functioning of other vital organs such as the kidney and liver also can be permanently compromised. "This drug is evil," says Penny, whose body was wrecked by a four-year meth addiction:

> Young people need to know that maybe for a minute you'll be skinny and full of energy, but the long-term effects are . . . I have no word to describe [it], but here is my story for young people to consider. It takes everything I have to walk a flight of stairs. My lungs are destroyed. I have no control over my bladder—I pee my pants all the time. I can't take a bowel movement without a laxative.[34]

Frightening Transformations in Appearance

Most of the damaging effects of meth on the brain, vital organs, and important bodily systems are invisible to the naked eye. But other symptoms of meth abuse can be quite visible. These frightening changes in physical appearance have become a centerpiece of anti-meth public education campaigns at both the state and federal levels.

Most people who manage to use meth every few weeks or months without developing full-blown addictions—and even

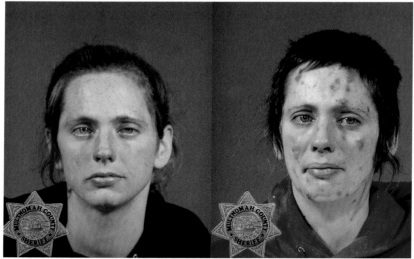

Before and after photos—taken six months apart—of a heavy meth user show the devastating effect the drug can have on the human body.

some regular users—are able to maintain their pre-meth physical appearance. For others, however, the signs of meth abuse become etched all over their bodies. One of the clearest indications of meth abuse is bad skin. Heavy meth use weakens and constricts blood vessels, which makes it more difficult for the body to pump blood to outer skin tissues. As a result, the skin loses its elasticity and its capacity to heal itself. Clusters of acne commonly afflict both teen and adult users of meth, and sores and scratches take much longer to disappear. This problem can be particularly severe for meth addicts who pick and scratch at themselves in search of imaginary crank bugs.

Another sign of meth addiction is extreme weight loss. Since people under the effects of meth typically lose their appetite and engage in extended bursts of frantic physical activity, they quickly shed pounds. Over time, however, heavy meth users can take on a gaunt, even anorexic appearance. "Some people I have in here over a hundred times, and I can look over a 10, 15, 20-year period and see how they've deteriorated, how they've changed," says a sheriff's deputy in Oregon. "Some were quite attractive when they began to come to jail: young people who were full of health and had everything going for them . . . and now they're a shell of what they once were."[35]

Meth Mouth

The most embarrassing physical side effect of heavy meth use, however, is the phenomenon known as meth mouth. Meth destroys teeth by drying up the mouth's salivary glands. These glands are vital because they produce fluids that neutralize naturally occurring acids and bacteria in the mouth. As saliva decreases, harsh acids and bacteria build up and begin eating away at teeth and gums. Other common symptoms of meth addiction are teeth grinding and cravings for sugary drinks, both of which can further damage teeth. Some heavy users of meth also stop paying attention to the basics of personal hygiene—including teeth brushing and flossing. Finally, financial problems sometimes keep meth addicts from seeking professional help for dental problems. All of these factors can combine to

Don Lance, a former drug user, displays one of the devastating effects of meth: rapid tooth decay and loss caused by the mouth's inability to create saliva.

turn the mouths of meth abusers into caverns of broken, rotted, and discolored teeth.

Some analysts of the meth trade believe that the threat of meth mouth has been exaggerated. "I've met all kinds of meth addicts," says journalist Nick Reding. "I've met very few meth addicts who don't have most of their teeth."[36] Some police officers, doctors, and dentists insist, however, that they have encountered the condition on multiple occasions. Health care professionals say that telltale signs of meth mouth can appear within a few months of heavy use of the drug. In the worst cases, the mouths of meth addicts can become so ruined that all of their teeth have to be removed and replaced with complete sets of dentures. "What I can tell you is what I have seen," says Stephen Wagner, a dentist who has treated a number of meth mouth cases. "It looks like someone has taken a hammer to these teeth and shattered them."[37]

Some dentists who have received visits from patients with meth mouth still express shock and wonderment at the extent of the damage caused by the drug. "I think every one of us [in the dental profession], when we see our first meth mouth, will sit back there with mixed emotions," says one dentist in Nebraska. "How in the world is this patient even functioning in such terrible pain? I can't think of anything that I've seen that can do as much damage to the mouth as quickly."[38]

These professional perspectives have been echoed by addicts who have fallen under meth's spell. A thirty-seven-year-old named Dolly recalls that her teeth decayed terribly during her addiction. But the drug had such a firm grip on her that she could not quit altogether. The most she could bring herself to do was switch from smoking meth to injecting it. "You asked me why I started shooting [meth]," she said. "It's what it was doing to my teeth. My teeth were falling apart. And I've always had good strong teeth. . . . and then when I was smoking that stuff, ooh. My teeth would just hurt. And they started disintegrating."[39]

METH'S TOLL ON FAMILIES AND COMMUNITIES

Methamphetamine has a well-deserved reputation for destroying the health, finances, and careers of individuals who become addicted to the drug. Addicts, though, are not the only people whose lives are scarred by meth. Marriages sometimes collapse under the strain of addiction, and the children of meth-addled parents are deprived of safe and secure childhoods. The wider community is affected as well. Meth abuse can put an enormous strain on law enforcement, foster care, and health care resources. Finally, the meth trade has diminished the feelings of safety, trust, and neighborliness that traditionally have been important elements of rural, small-town life.

Shattered Family Units

Meth addicts and cooks frequently express profound regret about the impact of their actions on members of their family. They admit that their addiction has caused terrible heartache for their parents, siblings, and spouses. This heartache stems not only from the sight of seeing a loved one take such a self-destructive path, but from the things that addicts do to feed their thirst for the drug. Many meth addicts have mournfully admitted to stealing money and property from family and friends to pay for their next dose, or "fix," of meth. Such betrayals can cause permanent damage to relationships. Some parents and siblings of addicts have sought to deal with their own emotional turmoil through involvement in Al-Anon and Nar-Anon. These national therapy and fellowship programs are designed specifically for friends and families of alcoholics and drug addicts, respectively.

Other meth users admit to having lured spouses, siblings, children, or other family members down the path of meth abuse. One mid-2000s report by the National Conference of State Legislatures found that 10 percent of meth users were introduced to the drug by parents or other relatives.[40]

"THEY WERE GOOD PARENTS, WHEN THEY WEREN'T HIGH"

"Half the time, [my little brothers and I] just ate snacks. There was lots of food. They just didn't fix us meals. That's when I think it was really bad. They'd sleep for days, get up and go to the bathroom and sleep again. They were good parents, when they weren't high."—MaKayla, the daughter of meth-addicted parents

Quoted in Erin Hoover Barnett. "Unnecessary Epidemic: Child of the Epidemic." *The Oregonian*, October 7, 2004. www.oregonlive.com/special/oregonian/meth/stories/index .ssf?1007_childofepidemic.html.

People who become entangled in the meth trade, whether as makers, dealers, or users (or all three), also place the financial health and security of their families in jeopardy. Meth cooks and meth users are at higher risk of suffering injuries ranging from burns from meth-making explosions to automobile accidents while driving under the influence. They also expose themselves to heart disease, kidney damage, and other long-term health problems that can be financially ruinous. This is especially true in poor and working-class households, many of which have limited or no health insurance to protect themselves against the high cost of hospital stays, medical procedures, and prescription drugs.

Families also suffer financially when job-holding members get in legal trouble for meth-related activities. "Meth users, dealers, and manufacturers who are apprehended, convicted and imprisoned generate human costs for themselves and for other family members," states one analysis of the economic impact of methamphetamine.

> The imposition of a prison sentence not only takes years out of the criminal's life, it leaves him or her with a permanent criminal record and strongly impacts the ability to . . . join the military or to pursue desired professional careers. Under some conditions, personal assets, such as

Ricky, a Kentucky meth lab explosion victim, received chemical burns over 40 percent of his body and suffers from chronic pain.

vehicles, houses and other personal valuables, obtained through meth profits may be confiscated and sold at public auction.[41]

In addition, many families spend tens of thousands of dollars to provide treatment for meth-addicted sons, daughters, or spouses. Many of these interventions are unsuccessful, or succeed only after months or years of money-draining efforts.

Lost Childhoods

Meth takes a particularly heavy toll on the most vulnerable family members: children. Young children of households under the shadow of meth often find that their parents' addiction leaves little money for fresh fruits and vegetables, new shoes or clothing, or enrollment in organized sports leagues or other recreational activities. Meth also strips them of healthy parental role models and deprives them of the sort of nurturing, supportive environment that helps them grow into productive members of society. "I've come across eight- or nine-year-old children who are able to describe to me how to make methamphetamine," says Betsy Dunn, a social worker with the Tennessee Department of Children's Services.

> They talk about "cooking the white stuff.". . . I can remember a case I worked last June, a little girl I removed [from her parents], her and her two brothers, when I explained to her she needed to come with me, she asked was it because of "that yucky smell that makes me feel sick." Even at that age, the children know that something is not right. I've had children tell me that a family outing meant going to this store to get this item, and going to another store to get that item. And they would tell me a list of ingredients used to make meth.[42]

Many individuals who are arrested and prosecuted for cooking, dealing, or using meth lose their parental rights. Their children are taken away by authorities for their own safety and placed in foster homes or in the care of other relatives. Meth-addicted

Colorado governor Bill Owens proposes legislation to protect children from meth labs in December 2002.

mothers and fathers who have lost legal custody of their own children frequently describe this experience as the worst thing to have ever happened to them. Yet some of them are still unable to kick their meth habits, even though they know it is their only chance to get their children back.

In the very worst cases, meth-addicted parents physically and emotionally abuse their children or expose them to toxic chemicals that can cause lasting damage to their developing bodies. This exposure is often a result of carelessness. Toddlers, for example, spend a lot of time crawling around on the floor, where meth residue or toxic drug-making chemicals often spill. But some meth cooks actually enlist their children as unpaid assistants in their operations. As investigative reporter Erin Hoover Barnett wrote in *The Oregonian*:

> Tens of thousands of children are suffering the consequences [of meth addiction]. . . . Many others are neglected while their parents get high, too distracted to attend to them. And they shuttle between relatives and

Meth's Impact on Infants and Young Children

Health researchers and medical professionals have expressed grave concerns about the health risks of meth to developing fetuses, infants, and young children. They say that pregnant women who use meth and parents who take or make the drug around their children are endangering the long-term mental health and physical well-being of their kids. Studies show that young children who inhale meth fumes, eat meth-contaminated foods, or receive meth-tainted blood and nourishment in the womb are more likely to suffer from asthma, insomnia, temper tantrums, depression, uncontrollable tremors, and a general inability to interact with other people. Researchers say, however, that it will be many years before they know whether childhood exposure to meth will lead to higher rates of heart and lung disease, high blood pressure, and other problems commonly experienced by adult meth users.

Kathryn M. Wells. "The Short- and Long-Term Medical Effects of Methamphetamine on Children and Adults." In *The Methamphetamine Crisis: Strategies to Save Addicts, Families, and Communities*, edited by Herbert C. Covey. Westport, CT: Praeger, 2007, pp. 57–74.

foster care, competing for their parents' affection against a cheap and plentiful drug, each time hoping that a child's love will prevail. It rarely does.[43]

Children's advocates worry that this mistreatment haunts many kids all the way into adulthood. "It's well established that the children who grow up in methamphetamine homes have significant [emotional] attachment disorders," says Melissa Haddow, a community organizer in Missouri:

The police will storm a house in hazmat [hazardous materials] suits with guns drawn, and the young children are so used to being ignored they don't even look up. These children are either terribly withdrawn or very aggressive, and they're going to grow up and follow the same path as their parents if we don't do something. It's a drug that doesn't just affect the user but has an incredible effect on the entire family unit.[44]

Meth Linked to Higher Crime Rates

When meth manufacturing and rates of meth addiction soared in the early and mid-2000s, law enforcement agencies in many rural communities noticed a corresponding increase in local crime rates. Police say that the linkage between the two developments was clear: as meth users exhausted their personal financial resources to feed their addictions, they turned to burglary, identity theft, and drug dealing to get more meth. Sometimes meth addicts stole automobiles, electronics, jewelry, or other items that could be sold on the black market. On other occasions, addicts grabbed anhydrous ammonia from remote farm fields or chemicals from local hardware stores and pharmacies to make their own batches. Drug experts agree that meth continues to fuel higher crime rates in towns and cities scattered across the country, especially in rural regions or urban neighborhoods where good-paying jobs are hard to find.

Law enforcement officials also say that the methamphetamine trade produces a steady stream of serious injuries and deaths. Explosions and fires at illegal meth labs are the most commonly cited source of these casualties, but emergency rooms also deal with meth overdoses and burns from exposure to meth-making chemicals. One Iowa physician recalls:

> One story among many of a boy who waited nearly two days to come to the emergency room following an incident while stealing anhydrous [ammonia] in which a small amount of the liquid had spilled on his jeans. He'd have come [to the hospital] sooner, but he was still high, and he didn't want to go to jail. By the time he got to the ER . . . one of the boy's testicles had melted off.[45]

Meth also breeds crimes of violence. Police say that meth kitchen operators sometimes resort to bloodshed to defend

Dealing with a Tweaker

The National Institute of Justice (the research arm of the U.S. Department of Justice) and various law enforcement and emergency health care organizations have issued guidelines for dealing with meth users who are tweaking—coming down from an extended drug high. These guidelines for police officers, emergency personnel, and family members include:

- Avoid shining bright lights on the tweaker, since light stimulation can be a violence trigger.

- Move slowly and keep hands visible to keep the tweaker calm.
- Engage the tweaker in conversation, as experts believe that tweakers who fall silent are more likely to act on paranoid thoughts and hallucinations.
- Maintain a distance of eight to ten feet from the tweaker so that he or she does not feel physically threatened.

Sandra B. McPherson, Harold V. Hall, and Errol Yudko. *Methamphetamine Use: Clinical and Forensic Aspects*. 2nd ed. Boca Raton, FL: CRC Press, 2011, p. xvi.

their sales territory or safeguard their facilities from discovery. Meth users also have been known to slide into deep pits of paranoia, hallucination, and aggression that make them more likely to lash out violently against friends, family members, or innocent strangers who cross their paths. Social workers, health care professionals, and police officers agree that homes where meth is consumed are at heightened risk of domestic violence.

Experts regard the meth addict who is tweaking as the most unpredictable and potentially dangerous type of user. Tweakers are addicts who become trapped in a state of paranoid, anxiety-riddled hyperactivity when they come down from a sleepless, multi-day meth high. This dangerous condition has been diagnosed in all types of meth users, but it is particularly common among crystal meth addicts. Many federal agencies and local police departments have issued special guidelines for officers, health care workers, and family members dealing with a tweaker.

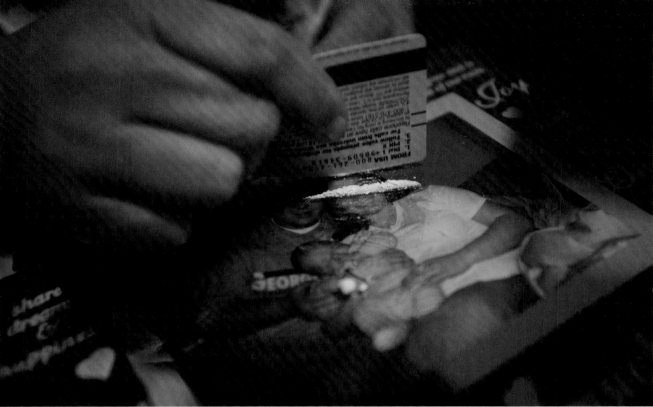

A line of meth is prepared to be snorted off of a photograph of a Kentucky family ravaged by meth use.

Inevitably, the problems that meth causes for families—tainted childhoods, shattered trust, damaged health, financial ruin, and prison time—also spill over into the wider community. Journalist Nick Reding interviewed Clay Hallberg, a physician in Oelwein, Iowa, who compared meth to brain cancer:

> Just as brain cancer often spreads to the lungs, said Clay [Hallberg], meth often spreads between classes, families, and friends. Meth's associated rigors affect the school, the police, the mayor, the hospital, and the town businesses. As a result, there is a kind of collective low self-esteem that sets in once a town's culture must react solely to a singular—and singularly negative—stimulus."[46]

A Financial Strain on Communities

Just as meth can drive a family into financial ruin, the drug can wreak havoc on the economic health and stability of communities. "Apart from the personal tragedies of meth abuse, counties have been forced to divert scarce tax dollars to address meth lab cleanups, jails overcrowded with individuals arrested for meth-related crimes, and rescuing innocent children from their meth-addicted parents and bringing them into the social services system,"[47] confirms one former president of the National Association of Counties.

Hospitals and other public health services are also financially vulnerable to meth epidemics. Meth patients can overwhelm emergency-care facilities and drug treatment and rehabilitation programs. This is especially true of hospitals and treatment programs in rural and inner-city areas, which treat a higher level of uninsured patients than facilities based in affluent neighborhoods and suburbs.

ABANDONED CHILDREN RAISED BY GRANDPARENTS

"Guess you've heard this story before: grandparents raising kids because their kid is on meth. Our daughter is almost 24, the mother of two beautiful boys—two perfect little boys who shine like stars in our daily lives. . . . I'll always love my daughter, but I don't love the woman who decided that meth was more important than her children."—grandparent caregiver of two children with a meth-addicted mother

Quoted in Generations United. *Meth and Child Welfare: Promising Solutions for Children, Their Parents and Grandparents.* Washington, DC: Generations United, 2006, p. i. www .gu.org/LinkClick.aspx?fileticket=qQzEk69Dnzs%3D&tabid=157&mid=606.

In the case of patients who need care for burns caused by meth lab fires, for example, the average cost of treatment in 2011 was $130,000 in hospital charges alone, according to an analysis conducted by a medical burn center in Kalamazoo, Michigan, as reported by the Associated Press.[48] This figure, which is about 60 percent higher than treatment costs for a typical burn victim, does not include additional expenses related to doctors' fees, rehabilitation, or plastic surgery. "Quite honestly, a lot of these [patients] don't have insurance," says the commander of one drug-fighting task force in Michigan. "This is coming out of the taxpayers' pockets to pay for these things."[49] Several burn wards across the United States have even been forced to shut their doors in recent years, in part because of the high expense of treating uninsured meth patients.

Meth's Environmental Impact

Meth operations also threaten the environmental health and well-being of the surrounding region. "Meth manufacturing is an environmental nightmare," declares the Arizona Attorney General's Office. "For every pound of meth that is made, five to

A bag of discarded meth-making waste is found in the woods by a narcotics enforcement team. The byproducts of meth production damage the environment.

six pounds of waste are generated. Those who make meth often dispose of waste by flushing it down toilets, putting it into the trash, dumping it on the ground, pouring it into waterways and leaving it in hotels or public storage facilities."[50]

When toxic byproducts of meth-cooking operations are dumped in nearby fields, streams, and forests, they can poison fish and other wildlife and disrupt local ecosystems for years. In some cases, this dumping can also jeopardize human health. Chemicals from meth kitchens that are introduced into local water supplies, for example, have sometimes contaminated crops raised for human consumption or livestock feed. Scientists warn that toxic waste from meth-cooking operations can linger in soil or groundwater supplies for years.

Environmental cleanup of buildings used for meth manufacturing operations puts additional financial strain on communities and states. Homes, apartments, garages, and sheds used for cooking meth absorb all kinds of potentially deadly chemicals into their walls and floors. Authorities have little choice but to undertake expensive cleanup efforts on these properties—often by hiring one of the many private companies that specialize in treating and restoring former meth-cooking facilities. The alternative is to leave neighborhoods and rural areas pocked with hazardous waste sites that endanger the health of neighbors and future occupants. In fact, cases have been documented from Maine to Oregon of families fighting mysterious illnesses who eventually discover that their homes were former meth lab sites.

CHAPTER 4

COMBATING THE METH INDUSTRY

In the 1990s and the first decade of the twenty-first century, lawmakers and law enforcement organizations took a variety of steps to fight back against the meth trade and protect communities from the devastating effects of meth addiction. Some of these measures, such as imposing tight restrictions on the sale of cold and flu medications that meth cooks use to make the drug, have been widely praised. Police, physicians, researchers, and legislators, however, are discussing additional measures to reduce the impact of meth on families and communities. These proposals range from local- and state-level programs to laws and initiatives of national and even international scope.

The Challenge of Controlling Precursor Chemicals

American law enforcement agencies and health care organizations admit that meth production is extremely difficult to stop. Since methamphetamine is a synthetic drug rather than one generated from a plant (such as cocaine or marijuana), crops of meth that can be seized or sprayed do not even exist. Instead, local, state, and federal law enforcement organizations are confronted with the task of keeping precursor chemicals used in meth making from ever reaching the hands of both large drug-trafficking organizations and small-time meth cooks.

This task is further complicated by the fact that many of the chemicals used to make meth actually have legitimate and lawful purposes. The two chemical ingredients that traditionally have

U.S. senator Dianne Feinstein holds a package of cold medicine at a news conference on tightened regulations for the sale of products that can be used to make meth.

been the foundation for meth recipes—ephedrine and pseudo-ephedrine—are also the main active ingredients in the country's best-known cold, flu, and allergy medicines.

The Combat Methamphetamine Epidemic Act, which was signed into law in 2006, reflects this fact. It was crafted by Congress to keep ephedrine and pseudoephedrine out of the hands of meth makers without hurting pharmaceutical companies or the millions of people who seek relief from allergies and colds every year. This law still permitted the sale of medicines containing pseudoephedrine, such as Sudafed and Nyquil, without a doctor's prescription. But the act included provisions to place these products behind pharmacy counters and impose limits on the amount of these medicines that customers could purchase.

A Shape-Shifting Foe

Since the federal Combat Meth Act was passed, many states— including Alabama, Florida, Hawaii, Illinois, Indiana, Iowa,

Kansas, Kentucky, Louisiana, Missouri, Nebraska, Oklahoma, North Carolina, North Dakota, South Carolina, Tennessee, Texas, and Washington—have introduced additional measures to monitor pseudoephedrine sales. Two states—Oregon and Mississippi—even passed laws requiring a doctor's prescription to purchase medicine containing pseudoephedrine. Authorities in both of these states subsequently reported a dramatic decline in the number of meth labs within their borders. After Oregon passed its law in 2006, for example, meth lab raids in the state dropped from 192 in 2005 to 7 by 2012. Mississippi reported that in-state meth lab seizures fell by 70 percent within a year of passing its own law in 2010.[51]

These results have convinced other states with significant meth problems, including Alabama, Missouri, and Oklahoma, to consider making pseudoephedrine-based drugs available only through prescription. Such proposals, however, face strong opposition from the U.S. pharmaceutical industry, which knows that prescription requirements reduce sales of profitable cold and allergy medicines.

METH ADDICTION OFTEN CLAIMS BOTH PARENTS

"In most cases of violence or abuse, a child may be removed from one parent. With meth, children often go into foster care because they lose both of their parents to the drug."—Dennis Sutton, CEO of the Children's Home Society of West Virginia

Quoted in Generations United. *Meth and Child Welfare: Promising Solutions for Children, Their Parents and Grandparents.* Washington, DC: Generations United, 2006, p. 10. www.gu.org/LinkClick.aspx?fileticket=qQzEk69Dnzs%3D&tabid=157&mid=606.

Local officials and health organizations have pitched in with their own meth-fighting efforts. These initiatives have included meth treatment programs, new neighborhood watch programs that emphasize identification of potential meth operations, and tax breaks for people who purchase and fix up abandoned

Meth Addiction Around the World

Methamphetamine trafficking is a problem all around the world. Meth and other amphetamine-type stimulants (ATSs) rank as the second most widely used class of drugs on the planet (behind marijuana). Some international health and drug enforcement agencies have estimated that there may be as many as 26 million meth addicts worldwide. Use of the drug is rising particularly fast in Asia. According to a 2012 report in *The Economist*, half of all drug takers seeking treatment for addiction in Japan have problems with meth, while in South Korea the proportion is even higher at 90 percent. By contrast, meth addicts account for only a small fraction of Americans and Europeans who enter narcotic abuse treatment programs.

Meth cartels are also gaining strength in such diverse parts of the world as West Africa, China, and the Czech Republic. As a result, law enforcement efforts against meth manufacturing operations have increased significantly.

"The Methamphetamine Business: Methed Up." *The Economist*, March 24, 2012. www.economist.com /node/21551026.

United Nations Office on Drugs and Crime (UNODC). *2013 World Drug Report*. www.unodc.org/unodc /secured/wdr/wdr2013/World_Drug_Report_2013 .pdf.

A villager in Myanmar uses yabaa, which is Thai for "madness drug" and is a form of methamphetamine.

buildings and other properties that might otherwise be used for meth labs.

Law enforcement authorities and meth industry experts say that all of these efforts are necessary, and that municipal, state, and federal officials will need to keep the pressure on for years to come. Stamping out meth will also require a willingness and ability to adapt to the ever-changing operations of meth labs. Meth traffickers who lose access to favored precursor chemicals such as pseudoephedrine have displayed a frustrating ability to switch to other precursors for their meth recipes. Since 2010, for example, meth traffickers have increasingly substituted pseudoephedrine with phenylacetone, which can be easily obtained in Mexico.

A pharmacist in Oregon holds a pseudoephedrine tablet in 2006, a few days before the state passed a law requiring a prescription for cold medicines containing the ingredient.

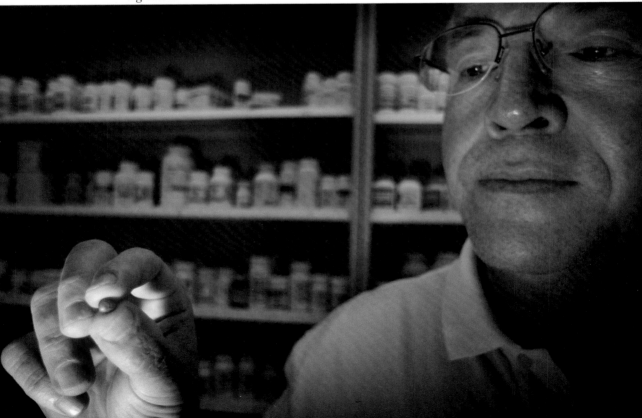

Drug enforcement officials lament the ability of meth manufacturers to respond to chemical shortages with new recipes that utilize other chemical substitutes. "The [meth] market gets crushed" when authorities take steps to cut off precursor supplies or make big meth lab busts, "but the bad guys retool with new chemicals, new formulas, and new routes,"[52] says Matt Nice of the International Narcotics Control Board (INCB), which implements drug policies of the United Nations.

Traffickers' skill in making meth from a multitude of recipes has led some observers to claim that meth will never be completely eradicated. "It's never going away," says Jane Maxwell, a research scientist at the University of Texas's Center for Social Work. "It's whack-a-mole."[53] Meth chemist Steve Preisler, who wrote a notorious meth cookbook in the 1980s under the name Uncle Fester, is also skeptical. He compares imposing "chemical restrictions" to stop meth production to "squeezing mud, the stuff just comes out between your fingers. . . . They make life difficult for the smurfers [small-time cooks who make meth for their own personal use] but for people with connections, well, they find [obtaining meth-making chemicals] to be no problem at all."[54]

A Global Effort

Law enforcement experts admit that meth traffickers have a knack for working around precursor chemical restrictions. Officials with the Drug Enforcement Administration (DEA) and other agencies assert, however, that nations increasingly are working together to limit the recipe options of meth makers and put steady pressure on their operations.

Authorities point out that international trade agreements have already forced meth traffickers to curtail their use of ephedrine and pseudoephedrine, which once formed the pillars of global meth production. In addition, international efforts to combat meth trafficking reportedly are getting increased support from governments in Southeast Asia and West Africa, where concerns about meth production and abuse are on the rise. Global orga-

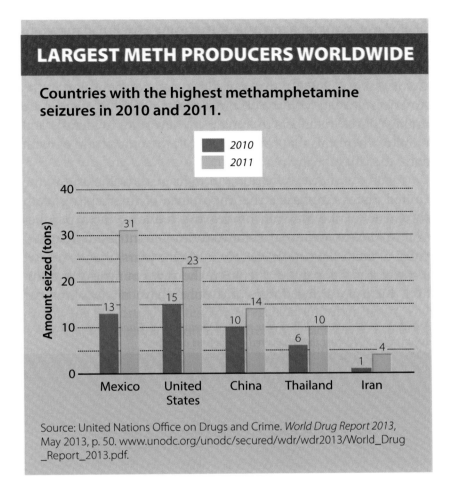

LARGEST METH PRODUCERS WORLDWIDE

Countries with the highest methamphetamine seizures in 2010 and 2011.

■ 2010
■ 2011

Amount seized (tons)

Mexico: 13, 31
United States: 15, 23
China: 10, 14
Thailand: 6, 10
Iran: 1, 4

Source: United Nations Office on Drugs and Crime. *World Drug Report 2013*, May 2013, p. 50. www.unodc.org/unodc/secured/wdr/wdr2013/World_Drug _Report_2013.pdf.

nizations such as the United Nations Commission on Narcotic Drugs (UNCND) and the International Narcotics Control Board are enlisting the support of these nations to implement policies that will reduce the worldwide manufacture, distribution, and use of known precursor chemicals.

Experts believe that one of the keys to combating meth is to establish international monitoring systems that can effectively track shipments of known precursor chemicals and block their sale before they can be diverted to meth production. The international community took important steps in this direction in 2010 and 2011, when the UNCND voted to tighten controls on

Television advertisement campaigns designed to educate society about the harmful effects of meth dependence; print and other news media articles about meth; public awareness efforts in the schools and public speaking by former meth addicts, including youth, and young people whose parents are meth users; community and state wide conferences; and Internet resources, including those specifically designed to target young people.[57]

Some anti-meth advertising campaigns in the United States have received national attention over the years. In 2004 the Multnomah County Sheriff's Office in Oregon launched a "Faces of Meth" campaign that used arrest record photographs of addicts to show how meth ravaged their physical appearance over time. These graphic ads became a model for similar campaigns by local, state, and national anti-drug groups.

THE BUSINESS PHILOSOPHY OF METH DEALERS

"At first we give [the meth] away. Then the addicts will do anything to get more."—a meth dealer in Idaho

Quoted in Nick Reding. *Methland: The Death and Life of an American Small Town.* New York: Bloomsbury, 2009, p. 7.

The use of shocking and disturbing imagery is also a centerpiece of the Meth Project's efforts to keep young people off the drug. The Meth Project was founded in Montana in 2005 by private citizens who became alarmed by meth's rising profile in the state. Since then, the group has blanketed the state with edgy, attention-grabbing television, radio, print, online, mobile, and social media advertisements that depict the risks of meth addiction.

The Montana Meth Project's in-your-face campaign has been widely credited with a dramatic reduction in meth use across the state. Youth counselors, teachers, parents, and law enforcement officials believe that the advertisements were particularly

CRYSTAL MESS

Buzz killer.

He's tweaking. His heart is racing, he's grinding his teeth, he's talking really fast and not making much sense. He thinks he's sexy and popular. And he's bumped up his risk of getting HIV by 400%.

Don't mess with crystal.
For help, visit crystalmess.net

This message brought to you by SF Dept. of Public Health HIV Prevention Program

HIGH RISK

Public health campaigns such as San Francisco, California's "Crystal Mess" use jarring imagery and statistics to sway young people from using the drug.

effective in keeping young people from experimenting with the drug. "These ads have changed the consciousness of an entire generation of teenagers," says Cascade County District Attorney John Parker. "The ads don't take a preachy tone. They don't talk down to the kids but they lay out in very graphic, very real terms how this can ruin lives."[58] In fact, results from the Montana Meth Project have convinced the group's leadership to expand the prevention program into Arizona, Colorado, Georgia, Hawaii, Idaho, and Wyoming.

Prevention campaigns also emphasize the importance of parental involvement in the lives of teens. Substance abuse counselors across the country hammer home the point that addiction to meth and other dangerous drugs is not a problem for young

Fighting Meth Addiction Through Science

Research scientists are reporting encouraging results in efforts to develop a vaccine against methamphetamine addiction. In November 2012, for example, scientists at The Scripps Research Institute (TSRI) in California announced that they had developed a vaccine that effectively inoculated laboratory rats against the narcotic chemicals contained in meth.[1]

The concept behind the work taking place at TSRI and other medical research facilities is to develop a vaccine capable of "turning on" an addict's immune system against meth and other addictive substances such as cocaine, heroin, and nicotine. Scientists believe

that if they can get immune systems to generate antibodies against the main chemical ingredients of various meth recipes, they can eradicate meth addiction. Meanwhile, scientists at the UCLA Center for Behavioral and Addiction Medicine in 2013 announced promising results for a new drug that seeks to reduce addicts' powerful craving for methamphetamine.[2]

1. Scripps Research Institute. "Meth Vaccine Shows Promising Results in Early Tests," Press release, November 1, 2012. www.scripps.edu/news/press/2012/20121 101taffe.html.

2. Kathleen Miles. "Meth Addiction Cure: UCLA Tests Ibudilast on Human Addicts." *Huffington Post*, April 3, 2013. www.huffingtonpost.com/2013/04/03 /meth-addiction-cure-ucla-ibudilast_n_2863126.html.

people who never experiment with the substances in the first place. Parents can be a huge help in this regard if they communicate openly with their teens. "Parents need to be tuned in to the dangers their kids are facing," said Peg Shea, who directed the Montana Meth Project from 2005 to 2008. "And they need to let their kids know they're willing to discuss the problem."[59]

Increased Investment in Meth Treatment Programs

Intervention programs for addiction are seen as another important tool in fighting methamphetamine. Substance abuse counselors, health professionals, and law enforcement authorities caution that kicking a meth addiction is extremely hard. They hasten to add, however, that some people who enter meth intervention and treatment programs eventually are able to walk

Addiction treatment centers such as this one in Cando, North Dakota, are crucial to the recovery of rural sufferers of meth addiction.

away from meth, reclaim their lives, and rebuild broken careers and family relationships.

Some of these intervention programs are made available through jails, prisons, halfway houses, and community centers. Faith-based organizations and other volunteer groups have played a crucial role in establishing and maintaining a number of these offerings. Other meth rehabilitation programs are maintained by commercial health care businesses that require financial compensation for their services.

One of the biggest obstacles to effective meth treatment is money. Many addicts and their families cannot afford enrollment in a private rehabilitation program or facility. But towns, counties, and states report that they do not have the financial resources to expand their meth treatment and recovery programs to meet demand. "All of this intervention takes money," says Chris

Smith, a sheriff in Canyon County, Idaho, "and there's just so much money to go around."[60]

Since drug treatment programs in the U.S. prison system are particularly limited, many substance abuse experts have urged policymakers and judges to direct meth abusers who get in trouble with the law (for nonviolent offenses) into community-based meth rehabilitation programs rather than jail cells. Experts assert that community treatment programs give abusers the opportunity to continue their careers and fulfill family obligations at the same time that they receive help in kicking their meth habits.

CHAPTER 5

Kicking Meth Addiction

For men, women, and teens trapped deep in methamphetamine addiction, the road to getting and staying "clean"—drug-free—is long and challenging. It is also never-ending. Like other people in recovery from addictions to cocaine, alcohol, tobacco, and heroin, former meth addicts must remain on guard against a relapse for the rest of their lives. Substance abuse experts and former meth abusers agree, though, that people trapped in the prison of meth addiction can escape. And once they are in a place of sobriety, often they can rebuild lives, careers, and family relationships that once seemed hopelessly lost.

Recognizing the Signs

The best way to beat meth is never to try it—a stance summed up by the anti-meth slogan "Not Even Once." In cases where the individual is already using meth on a semi-regular or regular basis, action should be taken to keep that experimentation from blowing up into full addiction. Parents, friends, and family members are all in a better position to intervene and get their loved ones the help they need if they can recognize the signs of meth use. These early warning signs, which can also signal experimentation with other illegal drugs, may include:

- Secretive behavior and avoidance of family and longtime friends
- Excessive sweating that does not appear to be from physical exertion or heat
- Dilated pupils and rapid eye movement

- Decreased appetite and sudden weight loss
- Increased anxiety and jittery bodily movements
- Extended bursts of talking
- Unusual or unpleasant body odor
- Sudden decrease in hours spent sleeping or at rest
- Burn marks around the mouth or on fingers
- Hidden drug paraphernalia, including plastic baggies (sometimes cut into triangles), playing cards or razor blades (used to crush crystal meth into powder), plastic straws and empty pen casings (used to snort meth), strips of aluminum foil, partially crushed soda cans with small punctures, butane cigarette lighters, light bulbs with the bottoms and filaments removed, glass smoking pipes (all used to smoke meth), and syringes and spoons with burn residue (used for injecting meth)

Dilated pupils can be one sign of meth use in addition to unusual body odor, jittery bodily movements, extended bursts of talking, or burn marks around the mouth or fingers.

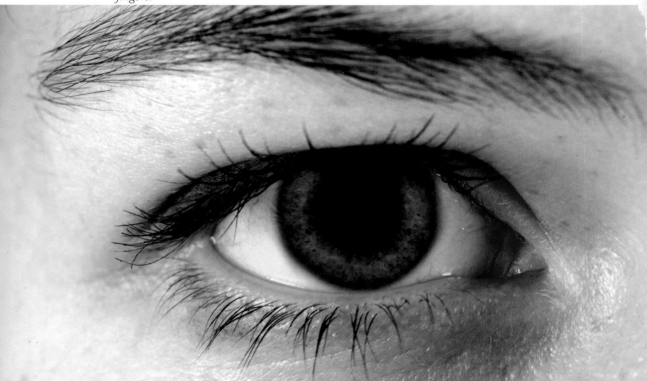

As meth takes a firmer grip on the user, common symptoms of addiction include:

- Significant declines in physical appearance, including bad teeth, poor skin (including sores), ratty hair, and unhealthy weight loss
- Obsessive picking and scratching at skin or hair
- Disinterest in maintaining basic personal hygiene
- Going days without sleep
- Obsession with completing repetitive tasks
- Requesting money and selling personal possessions
- Disappearance of valuable items or money from the home
- Angry emotional outbursts
- Intense paranoia and hallucinations

A Long Road Back

Candy Singer was a successful lawyer in Oregon before becoming addicted to methamphetamine. Within a matter of months, she was evicted from her apartment, her law practice fell apart, and she and her boyfriend—a meth dealer and fellow addict—began burglarizing homes, garages, and storage lockers to feed their habits.

After Candy was arrested for burglary and methamphetamine possession, her case was diverted to a special "drug court" that placed her on probation and enrolled her in a drug rehabilitation program. From that point on, Candy slowly battled her way out of addiction. But according to her sister, Thea Singer, the struggle was hard and long. "Candy was lucky in that our mother had both the funds and the drive to keep her in rehab as long as she needed it—almost two years, as it turned out. It took that long because, like other meth addicts, she essentially needed to fix the basic structure of her brain," says Thea. "The brain needs time to regenerate . . . before recovery can even start." Thea recalls that when Candy got her first job after beginning treatment, "my sister, the former lawyer, had to use a cheat sheet to operate the cash register at Pet Valu."

Thea Singer. "Recipe for Disaster." *Washington Post Magazine*, January 15, 2006. www.washingtonpost.com /wp-dyn/content/article/2006/01/11/AR2006011 102030.html.

Doctors and substance abuse experts urge families, friends, and teachers not to ignore or discount these symptoms, as troubling as they might be to consider. "It's natural for parents to want to believe their kids are innocent," says Minnesota drug abuse expert Carol Falkowski. "But if adults don't intervene, it will only cause the problem to escalate."[61]

Wendy Macker of Kalispell, Montana, intervened when her outgoing fifteen-year-old son Graham, a top student and athlete, turned into a virtual stranger over a period of a few months. He withdrew from his family, exchanged childhood friends for an unfamiliar crowd, and turned pale and moody. When Macker's jewelry was stolen in a burglary, she immediately suspected her troubled son. Determined to find out what was going on, she confronted one of Graham's new buddies. He told Macker that her son was regularly shooting up with methamphetamine.

Macker acted immediately and decisively. She forcibly put Graham in a six-month meth treatment program that gave him the strength and resources to get clean. "If she hadn't done that, meth would've killed me," Graham later said. "They call meth 'the devil,' and it brought out the devil in me. I stole from family and friends. I robbed houses. All I cared about was my next fix. . . . I still have cravings every day and attend support meetings every night. But life's worth living again. My mom thinks that's a miracle. I guess she's right."[62]

Treatment Options

A variety of treatment programs exist for methamphetamine addiction. The legal system maintains some programs for prison inmates and parolees. Funding for such efforts is limited, however, and many meth abusers in jail do not have access to this counseling. Some offenders are also sometimes placed in community-based substance abuse treatment programs, either as an alternative to jail or as a condition of their release from prison.

Abusers outside the criminal justice system have a wider variety of treatment options. The recovery support organizations Narcotics Anonymous and Crystal Meth Anonymous offer recovering meth addicts a free resource for fellowship and encouragement from other men and women who have struggled with addiction. Both of these organizations base their efforts on twelve-step addiction recovery programs and regular attendance at group meetings. "The group atmosphere provides help from peers and offers an ongoing support network for addicts who wish to pursue and maintain a drug-free lifestyle,"[63] explains the Narcotics Anonymous website.

Narcotics Anonymous and other recovery support groups can be helpful for recovering meth users.

Families struggling with a meth-addicted member may also turn to therapy programs that provide assistance in return for financial compensation. Some of these programs are tailored for outpatients, meaning that the patient continues to live at home while attending regular therapy sessions. Others rely on an inpatient or residential framework, in which the patient actually stays for a period of weeks or months at a rehabilitation center. These treatment options, which typically provide a blend of individual and family therapy, education, twelve-step support, and drug testing, have been shown to be effective in reducing methamphetamine abuse, according to the National Institute on Drug Abuse.[64]

THE THERAPEUTIC BENEFITS OF A CHILD'S LOVE

"To tell you the truth, if I didn't get help when I did, I would be dead. I've been sober one and a half years, and I've never felt better. I love myself again, and the happiness that I see in my son's eyes is the most amazing feeling I could ever have. That feeling has taken meth's place."—a mother in recovery from meth addiction

Quoted in Generations United. *Meth and Child Welfare: Promising Solutions for Children, Their Parents and Grandparents.* Washington, DC: Generations United, 2006, p. 6. www.gu.org/LinkClick.aspx?fileticket=qQzEk69Dnzs%3D&tabid=157&mid=606, p. 6.

For many families fighting to get a loved one off meth, however, these expensive treatment options are beyond their reach or taken only as a last resort. Many health insurance policies provide no coverage for such programs, while others only cover the expense for a few weeks. This is a big problem, as experts say that kicking a meth addiction can often take a year or more. Some individuals and families simply do not have the financial resources for these courses. Others manage to afford them, but only by making enormous financial sacrifices—such as exhausting hard-won retirement savings or selling a beloved home to pay for treatment.

The Long but Rewarding Road to Recovery

Judy Murphy of Ottumwa, Iowa, is the co-founder of the Moms Off Meth support group and a longtime meth treatment specialist. She is also a former meth abuser who spent the late 1980s and early 1990s drowning under the weight of addiction. First attracted to methamphetamine because it gave her an infusion of happiness and helped her lose weight, Murphy slid into a deep addiction that made it impossible for her to responsibly care for her young children. "I was so ashamed of myself," she recalls. "So I decided I was going to quit." But none of the addiction programs and treatment centers she tried worked out. Again and again she returned to meth. "I'd look at my life and feel bad," she says. "I would cry when I was sticking the needle in my arm. I just hated myself for it. I asked God to help me die."[65]

For Murphy, the moment of truth came when a judge took custody of her three children and forced her to enter another meth treatment program. "Judy knew she had to straighten out or she'd never get her kids back," writes journalist Fran Smith. "She attended meetings religiously, sobbed her heart out, and let women [in the program] who were already well down the road of recovery cheer her on. . . . Their faith inspired her to stick

Judy Murphy (center) is the founder of Moms Off Meth, a support group in Ottumwa, Iowa, that advocates for children of meth users.

with it: She's been clean and sober since September 22, 1995."[66] Murphy's sobriety not only enabled her to get her children back and resume her education, it also inspired her to pursue a career as a substance abuse recovery counselor. "I felt blessed to make it out of the hell I lived in so long," she explains. "I knew lots of people could feel as good as I now did."[67]

Meth Leads to Other Substance Abuse

"We focus on methamphetamines the most. We found out in a hurry that most addicts will use three or four different drugs at once. Some of them are so addicted to methamphetamines that they have to drink a certain beer when they're taking meth or they have to smoke a certain kind of marijuana. So, it's not just one drug when we're talking about methamphetamine addictions."—Substance abuse counselor Dana Schuck

Quoted in "Counseling Meth Addicts: What Works and What Doesn't." NOW on PBS, May 23, 2008. www.pbs.org/now/shows/421/meth-counseling.html .

Murphy's addiction story contains many common elements of meth abuse cases. Her experience not only shows how meth lures users in and devastates families, it also underscores how difficult it is to kick a meth habit and achieve sobriety. For many years, in fact, most health care professionals, substance abuse counselors, and law enforcement authorities viewed meth addicts as lost causes. They believed that meth addicts who tried to quit were doomed to relapse. But Murphy and others like her— people who beat their addictions and reclaimed their lives— have helped to change this perception.

Staying Clean and Avoiding Relapse

Nonetheless, meth addicts and substance abuse experts agree that recovering from meth addiction is immensely difficult and takes a long time. "Meth effects can last up to six months for just one use, and the drug can do greater damage to a person's physical, behavioral, and thinking functions than many other illicit drugs or alcohol," according to University of Iowa researchers. "For this reason, it takes much longer to treat a person with a meth addiction than it does to treat someone with a cocaine or heroin problem."[68]

The cornerstone of meth treatment is behavioral therapy. This form of counseling seeks to steer abusers away from people, situations, and attitudes that trigger their meth use. It also helps people in recovery develop healthier methods for dealing with life's challenges and gives them tools to cope with their cravings. In some cases, recovering meth addicts also receive prescriptions for legal medications to help them deal with feelings of depression or anxiety that often follow withdrawal from the drug.

Trina Everhart (left), a recovered meth user, helps her sons with their homework. Family can be one of the most important support structures for recovering users.

Substance abuse experts emphasize that recovering addicts are less likely to relapse if they have a strong support network. Many family members and friends—even those who have been badly hurt by a loved one's addiction—stand ready to help. "My wife and I have done all we can to support our son during his battle with addiction," writes Dean Dauphinais, the father of a recovering heroin addict:

> We refuse to give up on our son. We also support our son by working on our recovery: going to Al-Anon and Nar-Anon meetings, going to therapy, going to family programs at rehab facilities; these are all ways we've tried to help our son by helping us. Addiction is a family disease, and the whole family needs to be treated.[69]

Another key for meth users trying to get clean is to develop and stick to a plan that keeps them away from social settings where the drug is available. Instead, people in recovery need to seek out environments that make it easier to stay clean. "One of the things we talk about, with probation, parole, and also our [prison] programs, is coming up with a plan before they get out," says Dana Schuck, a drug abuse counselor in Idaho:

> If they don't have a plan before they get out, statistics say 76 percent of people will use within 72 hours. That tells you how important it is to have a plan the day you get out. That's seeing your parole officer, having a place to live, finding a job, it's getting some good food to eat. It's going to Alcoholics Anonymous and Narcotics Anonymous those three days to get you bridged into another sphere of influence in your life that will help you in a positive way.[70]

Taking Heart from Inspiring Stories

Even addicts who take all these steps face a long and daunting journey to recovery. An Australian study published in 2012 in the journal *Addiction* found that 88 percent of meth addicts

A Former Addict's "Wish List"

Nic Sheff became addicted to methamphetamine as a teenager, and his life quickly spiraled out of control. Years of misery and heartbreak followed, but he finally was able to kick his habit, get married, and build a career as a writer. His credits include two memoirs about his meth addiction, *Tweak* and *We All Fall Down*. Sheff is grateful for his life of sobriety, but he says that he will always regret the pain that his meth addiction unleashed on his family:

> I did terrible things—stealing, breaking in to people's houses, lashing out at my family and loved ones, costing my parents tens of thousands of dollars in treatment costs. Not to mention all the damage I did to myself. . . . I missed out on so much of life. . . . I wish I had taken advantage of the opportunities that were given to me. I wish I'd never put my family through all that pain and suffering. I wish my sister hadn't lived her whole life with the shadow of my addiction looming over her. Because it is ever present. As much as I try to escape it, it is there with me always.

Nic Sheff. "I Shall Regret the Past." TheFix.com, October 2, 2012. www.thefix.com/content/we-shall-regret-the-past-11103.

who entered residential rehabilitation programs suffered relapses within three years of undergoing treatment.[71] Meth addicts who went through short-term substance abuse programs or quit with no professional help at all were even more likely to relapse. These results show the importance of sticking with therapy and rehabilitation programs long after users have kicked their meth habits. "Some people really have trouble grasping the fact that they need help for a longer period of time," says Richard Rawson, a substance abuse expert and professor at UCLA. "They want to go into rehab, get fixed, and go on with their life."[72]

These findings also show how important it is for individuals and families struggling with methamphetamine to hear stories of other substance abusers who have made lasting recoveries and constructed productive, rewarding, and happy lives. This is a

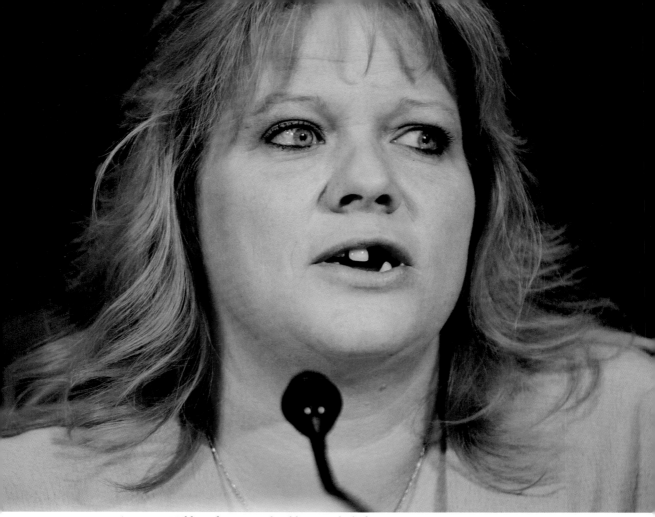

Aaronette Noble, a former meth addict, speaks before a U.S. Senate committee in 2006 about the devastating effects of meth, such as her tooth loss.

major focus of groups such as Narcotics Anonymous, Alcoholics Anonymous, and other organizations working to help people free themselves from drug and alcohol addiction. These groups know that such stories can inspire and give strength to people recovering from addiction.

The drug and alcohol treatment provider Foundations Recovery Network, for example, has created a website called Heroes in Recovery that encourages former drug and alcohol abusers to share their stories of triumph over addiction. Hundreds of people have contributed to the website, including a former meth addict named Tar who compares his life to a garden. "Before [my recovery from meth] my garden was dirty, weedy, rotten and not taken care of. But with a lot of work, water, weeding, and cultivating I have a beautiful harvest. As long as I keep it that way, it will continue to be beautiful."[73]

Chapter 1: The History of Methamphetamine

1. Nicolas Rasmussen. "America's First Amphetamine Epidemic, 1929–1971." *American Journal of Public Health* 98, no. 6 (2008): pp. 974–985. www.ncbi.nlm.nih.gov /pmc/articles/PMC2377281.

2. Olivia Dahl. "Psychostimulants: Cocaine for Toothaches and Amphetamines for All-nighters." *Dartmouth Undergraduate Journal of Science*, May 29, 2013. http://dujs.dartmouth .edu/spring-2013-15th-anniversary-edition/psychostimu lants-cocaine-for-toothaches-and-amphetamines-for-all -nighters#.UcH5bJxc25U.

3. Quoted in Bob Roehr. "Meth, Myth, and America." *Bay Area Reporter*, August 25, 2005. www.ebar.com/news/article.php ?article=99&sec=news.

4. Jack Shafer. "Meth Madness at Newsweek." Slate, January31,2007.www.slate.com/articles/news_and_politics/press _box/2005/08/meth_madness_at_newsweek.html.

5. "Timeline: The Meth Epidemic." *FRONTLINE: The Meth Epidemic*. PBS, May 2011. www.pbs.org/wgbh/pages/frontline /meth/etc/cron.html.

6. Nick Reding. *Methland: The Death and Life of an American Small Town*. New York: Bloomsbury, 2009, pp. 59, 69.

7. Reding. *Methland*, pp. 18, 64.

8. Reding. *Methland*, p. 69.

9. Fox Butterfield. "Across Rural America, Drug Casts a Grim Shadow." *New York Times*, January 4, 2004. www.nytimes .com/2004/01/04/us/across-rural-america-drug-casts-a grim-shadow.html?pagewanted=all&src=pm.

10. Quoted in Reding, p. 240.

11. Quoted in Susan Abram. "Meth Lab Busts Are Down by 40% in State." *Los Angeles Daily News*, June 20, 2006. www

.dailynews.com/general-news/20060620/meth-lab-busts
-are-down-by-40-in-state.

12. Quoted in Jonann Brady. "In the Trenches of the War on
Meth." ABCNews.com, November 2, 2005. http://abcnews
.go.com/Health/Drugs/story?id=1230527&page=2#
.UdsOFm1c25U.

13. Quoted in Associated Press. "Mexican Cartels Fill Demand
for Meth in USA." *USA Today*, October 11, 2012. www
.usatoday.com/story/news/nation/2012/10/11/mexico
-cartels-meth/1626383.

14. Jim Salter. "Mexico Drug Cartels Flood Cheap Meth into
U.S." *Huffington Post*, October 11, 2012. www.huffington
post.com/2012/10/11/mexico-drug-cartels-meth_n
_1957378.html.

15. Damien Cave. "Mexico Seizes Record Amount of Methamphetamine." *New York Times*, February 9, 2012. www
.nytimes.com/2012/02/10/world/americas/mexico-seizes
-15-tons-of-methamphetamine.html?_r=0.

16. Quoted in Ioan Grillo. "Mexican Meth Production Goes
on Speed." Reuters, May 10, 2012. www.reuters.com
/article/2012/05/10/us-mexico-drugs-meth-idUS
BRE84908820120510.

17. Substance Abuse and Mental Health Services Administration. "Highlights: Illicit Drug Use." *Results from the 2011
National Survey on Drug Use and Health: Summary of National Findings*. Rockville, MD: Substance Abuse and Mental Health Services Administration, 2012. www.samhsa.gov
/data/NSDUH/2k11Results/NSDUHresults2011.htm#LOT.

18. L.D. Johnston et al. *Monitoring the Future: National Results
on Drug Use: 2012 Overview Key Findings on Adolescent Drug
Use*. Ann Arbor: Institute for Social Research, University
of Michigan, 2013, p. 31. www.monitoringthefuture.org
/pubs/monographs/mtf-overview2012.pdf.

19. Jonah Engle. "Merchants of Meth: How Big Pharma Keeps
the Cooks in Business." *Mother Jones*, July/August 2013.
www.motherjones.com/politics/2013/08/meth-pseudo
ephedrine-big-pharma-lobby.

20. Quoted in Grillo. "Mexican Meth Production."

Chapter 2: Meth's Toll on Users

21. "Understanding Meth: How Meth is Made." Office of Illinois Attorney General. www.illinoisattorneygeneral.gov /methnet/understandingmeth/basics.html#Anchor -Ho-43198.

22. Associated Press. "Mexican Cartels Fill Demand for Meth in USA."

23. Gil Reavill. *Aftermath, Inc.: Cleaning Up After the CSI Goes Home*. New York: Gotham, 2007, p. 21.

24. Quoted in Veronique Lacapra. "'Shake-and-Bake' Meth Causes Uptick in Burn Victims." NPR: All Things Considered, February 7, 2012. www.npr.org/2012/02/07/146531937 /shake-and-bake-meth-causes-uptick-in-burn-victims.

25. "The Meth Epidemic: Transcript." *FRONTLINE: The Meth Epidemic*. PBS, May 2011. www.pbs.org/wgbh/pages/frontline /meth/etc/script.html.

26. Quoted in Jeremy Sare. "Addiction: Next Year's Drug." *New Statesman*, February 28, 2008. www.newstatesman.com /society/2008/02/drug-meth-addiction-users.

27. Quoted in Julie Mehta. "Dark Crystal: Meet Three Young People Who Got Swept Up in Meth Madness." *Current Health 2*, November 2005, p. 16.

28. Reding. *Methland*, p. 52.

29. Quoted in Mehta. "Dark Crystal," p. 16.

30. "Costs of Meth: Economics of Meth." Department of Criminal Justice and Sociology, Southeast Missouri State University. www.semo.edu/criminaljustice/costs_of_meth.htm.

31. Editors of *The Oregonian*. "Unnecessary Epidemic: Effects of Methamphetamine on the User." *The Oregonian*, October 7, 2004. www.oregonlive.com/special/oregonian/meth /stories/index.ssf?effects.html.

32. Quoted in "The Meth Epidemic: Transcript."

33. Thea Singer. "Recipe for Disaster." *Washington Post Magazine*, January 15, 2006. www.washingtonpost.com/wp-dyn /content/article/2006/01/11/AR2006011102030.html.

34. Quoted in Dirk Johnson. *Meth: The Home-Cooked Menace*. Center City, MN: Hazelden, 2005, p. 126.

35. Quoted in "How Meth Destroys the Body." *FRONTLINE:*

The Meth Epidemic. PBS, May 2011. www.pbs.org/wgbh /pages/frontline/meth/body/#3.

36. Quoted in interview with Benjamin Whitmer. INDenver-Times, 2009. www.methlandbook.com/interviews/from-in denver-times-part-two-of-a-two-part-interview.

37. Quoted in Monica Davey. "Grisly Effect of One Drug: 'Meth Mouth.'" *New York Times,* June 11, 2005. www.nytimes .com/2005/06/11/national/11meth.html?pagewanted=all.

38. Quoted in Trisha Schulz. "Meth Mouth Leaves Dentists 'Floored' by What They See." *Norfolk Daily News,* December 9, 2006. http://norfolkdailynews.com/news/meth -mouth-leaves-dentists-floored-by-what-they-see /article_5337899d-02cd-5898-b332-c7aa92c8f247 .html?mode=jqm.

39. Quoted in Miriam Boeri. *Women on Ice: Methamphetamine Use Among Suburban Women.* New Brunswick, NJ: Rutgers University Press, 2013, pp. 91–92.

Chapter 3: Meth's Toll on Families and Communities

40. Devonne R. Sanchez and Blake Harrison. "The Methamphetamine Menace." *Legisbrief* 12, no. 1 (January 2004). National Conference of State Legislatures. www.popcenter.org /problems/meth_labs/PDFs/Sanchez&Harrison_2004.pdf.

41. "Cost to the User and the User's Family." Department of Criminal Justice and Sociology, Southeast Missouri State University. www.semo.edu/criminaljustice/costs_of_meth .htm.

42. Quoted in Frank Owen. *No Speed Limit: The Highs and Lows of Meth.* New York: St. Martin's, p. 207.

43. Erin Hoover Barnett. "Unnecessary Epidemic: Child of the Epidemic." *The Oregonian,* October 7, 2004. www.oregon live.com/special/oregonian/meth/stories/index.ssf?1007 _childofepidemic.html.

44. Quoted in Owen. *No Speed Limit,* p. 199.

45. Reding. *Methland,* p. 35.

46. Reding. *Methland,* p. 73.

47. Quoted in Jim Philipps. "Methamphetamine Epidemic Rages On." *American City and County,* November 1, 2007.

http://americancityandcounty.com/pubsafe/government
_methamphetamine_epidemic_rages.

48. Associated Press. "Meth Fills Hospitals with Burn Patients."
USA Today, January 23, 2012. http://usatoday30.usatoday
.com/news/nation/story/2012-01-23/meth-burns-hospital
/52759026/1.

49. Quoted in Dan Armstrong. "Meth Burns Cost Taypayers."
MiNBCNews.com, January 23, 2012. www.minbcnews.com
/news/story.aspx?id=711004#.UfPA-W1c25U.

50. "Environmental Impact of Meth." Office of Arizona Attorney General Tom Horne. www.azag.gov/meth#environment
al_impact.

Chapter 4: Combating the Meth Industry

51. Glenn Smith. "Meth Lab Menace Grows Across South,
Straining State Resources." *Post and Courier,* July 20, 2013.
www.postandcourier.com/article/20130720/PC1610
/130729878.

52. Quoted in "The Methamphetamine Epidemic: Methed
Up." *The Economist*, March 24, 2012. www.economist.com
/node/21551026.

53. Quoted in Don Wade. "Meth Mayhem: Drug Trade Shifts to
Cartels, 'One-Pot' Cooks." Scripps-Howard News Service,
November 19, 2012. www.commercialappeal.com/news
/2012/nov/18/meth-mayhem-home-invasion.

54. Quoted in David W. Koop. "Old School Meth: Mexican Cartels Go Back to Basics." Associated Press, December 14, 2009.
www.boston.com/news/world/latinamerica/arti
cles/2009/12/14/old_school_meth_mexican_cartels_go
_back_to_basics.

55. Quoted in Paul Clinton. "U.S. Gives $12M to Mexico to
Combat Meth." *Police: The Law Enforcement Magazine*, August 23, 2012. www.policemag.com/channel/gangs/news
/2012/08/23/u-s-gives-12m-to-mexico-to-combat-meth
.aspx.

56. *The Oregonian* Editorial Board. "Mexico's Meth Haul." Ore
gonlive.com, February 12, 2012. www.oregonlive.com/op
inion/index.ssf/2012/02/mexicos_meth_haul.html.

57. Generations United. *Meth and Child Welfare: Promising Solutions for Children, Their Parents and Grandparents*. Washington, DC: Generations United, 2006, p. 1. www.gu.org /LinkClick.aspx?fileticket=qQzEk69Dnzs%3D&tabid=157 &mid=606.

58. Quoted in Ben Tracy. "Graphic Ads Turn Around Montana Teen Meth Use." CBSNews.com, September 20, 2011. www.cbsnews.com/8301-18563_162-20109143.html.

59. Quoted in Meredith Maran. "Getting Real about Meth." *Family Circle*, February 2009. www.familycircle.com/teen /drugs/getting-real-about-meth/?page=1.

60. Quoted in "Meth and Crime: A Sheriff's Insight." *NOW on PBS*. PBS, May 23, 2008. www.pbs.org/now/shows/421 /meth-crime.html.

Chapter 5: Kicking Meth Addiction

61. Quoted in Meredith Maran. "Getting Real about Meth." *Family Circle*, February 2009. www.familycircle.com/teen/drugs /getting-real-about-meth/?page=1.

62. Quoted in Maran. "Getting Real about Meth."

63. "Information about NA." Narcotics Anonymous, 2013. www.na.org/?ID=PR-index.

64. National Institute on Drug Abuse. "Methamphetamine." NIDA InfoFacts, March 2010. www.drugabuse.gov/sites/ default/files/methamphetamine10.pdf.

65. Quoted in Fran Smith. "Back from the Brink." *Redbook*, December 2007, p. 178. www.redbookmag.com/health-well ness/advice/back-from-the-brink.

66. Smith. "Back from the Brink."

67. Quoted in Smith. "Back from the Brink."

68. Quoted in "UI Researchers Urge Advances in Meth Abuse Treatment." University of Iowa News Services press release, August 14, 2003. www.news-releases.uiowa.edu/2003/aug ust/081403meth-abuse.html.

69. Dean Dauphinais. "Guest Blog." Heroes in Recovery, August 23, 2012. www.heroesinrecovery.com/blog/2012/08 /23/guest-blog-dean-dauphinais.

70. Quoted in "Counseling Meth Addicts: What Works and

What Doesn't." *NOW on PBS*, May 23, 2008. www.pbs.org /now/shows/421/meth-counseling.html.

71. Kerry Grens. "Detox, Rehab Keep Few Meth Users Clean Long Term." Reuters, August 1, 2012. www.reuters.com /article/2012/08/01/us-detox-rehab-idUSBRE8700WJ2 0120801.

72. Quoted in Grens. "Detox, Rehab Keep Few Meth Users Clean Long Term."

73. Quoted in "Tar." Heroes in Recovery, July 16, 2012. www .heroesinrecovery.com/stories/tar.

Chapter 1: The History of Methamphetamine

1. How were methamphetamine and other types of amphetamines legally used in the 1940s and 1950s? Who were the primary consumers of these drugs at that time?

2. What factors contributed to the development of "homebrewed" meth manufacturing operations in rural American communities in the 1980s and 1990s?

3. What steps have lawmakers taken to stop the diversion of legitimate cold and flu medicines into the meth trade?

Chapter 2: Meth's Toll on Users

1. What is the "shake and bake" method and why is it so popular among meth users?

2. Why is meth so addictive?

3. Tweaking and meth mouth are both signs of meth addiction. Explain what each of these terms means.

Chapter 3: Meth's Toll on Families and Communities

1. Discuss three reasons why meth addiction can have such a terrible impact on families.

2. Explain the linkage between meth addiction and higher crime rates.

3. What are some of the environmental and public health impacts of meth manufacturing operations?

Chapter 4: Combating the Meth Industry

1. Why have restrictions on precursor chemicals used to make meth had only limited success?

2. What are some of the features of effective anti-meth education efforts?

3. What is the "Faces of Meth" campaign?

Chapter 5: Kicking Meth Addiction

1. Name the early warning signs of possible meth abuse.

2. Discuss three different types of treatment options that meth addicts can turn to in order to get clean.

3. What are three keys for recovering meth addicts to avoid a relapse?

ORGANIZATIONS TO CONTACT

Crystal Meth Anonymous

4470 West Sunset Boulevard, Suite 107 PMB 555
Los Angeles, CA 90027-6302
phone: (855) 638-4373
website: www.crystalmeth.org

Crystal Meth Anonymous is a twelve-step program of fellowship for men and women fighting to recover from addiction to crystal meth. As the organization states, "the only requirement for membership is a desire to stop using."

Faces and Voices of Recovery

1010 Vermont Avenue, NW, Suite 618
Washington, DC 20005
phone: (202) 737-0690
fax: (202) 737-0695
website: facesandvoicesofrecovery.org

This national nonprofit group seeks to educate and mobilize Americans about the nature of alcohol and drug addiction and to provide resources for individuals and families seeking to end their abuse of alcohol or narcotics and stay on a path of recovery.

Narcotics Anonymous (NA)

P.O. Box 9999
Van Nuys, CA 91409
phone: (818) 773-9999
fax: (818) 700-0700
website: www.na.org

Narcotics Anonymous (NA) is an addiction recovery program with chapters all across the United States and around the world.

NA treatment efforts pivot around group meetings of individuals working toward lives of sobriety from drugs and alcohol.

Partnership for Drug-Free Kids

352 Park Avenue South, 9th Floor
New York, NY 10010
phone: (855) 378-4373; (212) 922-1560
fax: (212) 922-1570
website: www.drugfree.org

This influential, high-profile nonprofit group uses advertising and educational resources and information to prevent substance abuse by kids and to help parents, caregivers, and community leaders develop teen and young adult programs against drug and alcohol abuse.

Phoenix House

Phoenix House New York
164 West 74th Street, 4th Floor
New York, NY 10023
phone: (888) 286-5027
website: www.phoenixhouse.org

This well-known nonprofit anti-drug organization, which maintains dozens of addiction recovery programs in ten states and Washington, DC, focuses on treating and preventing drug and alcohol abuse in adults and teens. The Phoenix House website contains complete contact information for each chapter in the organization's network.

Students Against Destructive Decisions (SADD)

255 Main Street
Marlborough, MA 01752
phone: (877) 723-3462
fax: (508) 481-5759
website: www.sadd.org

SADD is a national peer-to-peer youth organization dedicated to keeping young people from abusing alcohol and drugs and engaging in other risky and destructive behaviors. Through SADD chapters in middle and high schools and colleges, young people themselves offer education and prevention programs in schools and communities.

Books

Miriam Boeri. *Women on Ice: Methamphetamine Use Among Suburban Women*. New Brunswick, NJ: Rutgers University Press, 2013. This work examines the United States' meth epidemic through in-depth and gripping interviews with a specific subsection of meth addicts—women in the nation's suburbs.

Generations United. *Meth and Child Welfare: Promising Solutions for Children, Their Parents and Grandparents*. Washington, DC: Generations United, 2006. This handbook produced by a nonprofit community development organization (and available at www.gu.org/LinkClick.aspx?fileticket=qQzEk69Dnzs%3D&tabid=157&mid=606) summarizes the disastrous consequences of meth addiction and makes the case for increased investment in drug treatment programs that can rebuild meth-damaged families.

David Sheff. *Clean: Overcoming Addiction and Ending America's Greatest Tragedy*. New York: Eamon Dolan, 2013. In this acclaimed follow-up to *Beautiful Boy* (a memoir about his son's struggle to overcome methamphetamine addiction), Sheff argues for wide-ranging legal, social, and medical reforms to the United States' approach to drug addiction. He asserts that Americans need to see drug and alcohol addiction as a treatable disease rather than a moral failing.

Articles

Jonah Engle. "Merchants of Meth: How Big Pharma Keeps the Cooks in Business." *Mother Jones*, July–August 2013. www.motherjones.com/politics/2013/08/meth-pseudoephedrine-big-pharma-lobby. The author of this investigative article argues that laws that require a doctor's prescription to buy cold or allergy medications are very effective in reducing meth production, but that big drug and pharmacy companies are sabotaging these proposals in order to protect their profits.

Megan McArdle. "Do We Need Even Tighter Controls on Sudafed?" Atlantic.com, February 6, 2012. www.theatlantic .com/health/archive/2012/02/do-we-need-even-tighter -controls-on-sudafed/252637. Many meth experts have urged the passage of laws that would require prescriptions for the purchase of cold and allergy medicines containing meth ingredients, but this essay argues that such measures unfairly punish innocent people fighting colds, allergies, and sinus infections.

Websites

The Fix (thefix.com). This website serves as a massive clearing-house of information on addiction and recovery issues, while also providing commentary, interviews, and analysis from drug experts and people in recovery from drug and alcohol addiction. This is a good resource for both teens and parents seeking help with family substance abuse problems.

FRONTLINE: The Meth Epidemic (www.pbs.org/wgbh/pages /frontline/meth). This Public Broadcasting System (PBS) website provides a wide range of information on meth addiction that *FRONTLINE* producers used in 2006 and 2011 reports on the issue. Materials available on the website include the full video of the 2011 investigative report on meth abuse broadcast by *FRONTLINE*; interviews with drug experts, counselors, and recovering addicts; frequently asked questions about meth addiction; a story on the "Faces of Meth" education campaign; and the transcript of the 2006 program. (Please be aware that information about state laws reported on the site may have changed since the original broadcasts.)

The Meth Project: Not Even Once (www.methproject.org). This informative website, created and maintained by the well-known Meth Project organization, provides a wide range of information on meth addiction and a variety of educational materials aimed at preventing meth abuse. It also includes links to more than a dozen anti-meth videos produced by the Meth Project.

Unnecessary Epidemic: A Special Investigative Report by *The Oregonian* (www.oregonlive.com/special/oregonian/meth). When this five-part investigative series spearheaded by *Oregonian* reporter Steve Suo was first published in 2004, it sparked a massive wave of stories on methamphetamine abuse from national news outlets. This website contains the full text of the *Oregonian* series as well as other supplementary features.

Videos

World's Most Dangerous Drug. National Geographic, 2006 (http://channel.nationalgeographic.com/channel/explorer/videos/worlds-most-dangerous-drug). This fifty-minute video from National Geographic provides an informative and graphic description of meth addiction and the emotional, physical, and financial toll that it can take on users.

INDEX

PICTURE CREDITS

Cover: © Oleg Golovnev/Shutterstock.com
© AFP/Getty Images, 27
© Andy Cross/Denver Post via Getty Images, 49
© AP Photo/Bruno González, 64
© AP Photo/Charlie Neibergall, 77
© AP Photo/Dave Kolpack, 69
© AP Photo/John Madill, 23
© AP Photo/PRNewsFoto/Templin Brink Design, 67
© AP Photo/Rick Bowmer, 61
© AP Photo/Sue Ogrocki, 30
© AP Photo/The Missoulian, Michael Gallacher, 79
© AP Photo/Wayne Maris, 19
© Barcroft Media via Getty Images, 42
© Gale, Cengage Learning, 26, 63
© Harvey Lloyd/Photolibrary/Getty Images, 13
© Jonathan Torgovnik/Getty Images, 47, 53
© Kallista Images/Getty Images, 10
© Lyn Alweis/Denver Post via Getty Images, 32
© MCT via Getty Images, 43
© MedicImage/Alamy, 72
© Mira/Alamy, 75
© NY Daily News via Getty Images, 7
© Phil Walter/Getty Images, 15
© Richard Pipes/Albuquerque Journal/ZUMAPRESS.com/Alamy, 34
© Shawn Ehlers/WireImage/Getty Images, 37
© Thierry Falise/LightRocket via Getty Images, 60
© Tim Dominick/The State/MCT via Getty Images, 55
© Tom Williams/Roll Call/Getty Images, 58
© Visuals Unlimited, Inc./Science VU/Getty Images, 39
© William F. Campbell/Time & Life Pictures/Getty Images, 36
© Win McNamee/Getty Images, 82

ABOUT THE AUTHOR

Kevin Hillstrom is an independent scholar who has written numerous books on American history, environmental and social issues, and U.S. politics and policy.